LOUD

DREW AFUALO

LO

ACCEPT NOTHING LESS THAN THE
LIFE YOU DESERVE

AUWA BOOKS

MCD | FARRAR, STRAUS AND GIROUX | NEW YORK

AUWA Books
MCD / Farrar, Straus and Giroux
120 Broadway, New York 10271

Copyright © 2024 by Drew Afualo Enterprises, LLC
All rights reserved
Printed in the United States of America
First edition, 2024

Library of Congress Cataloging-in-Publication Data
Names: Afualo, Drew, 1995– author.
Title: Loud : accept nothing less than the life you deserve / Drew Afualo.
Description: First edition. | New York : AUWA Books / MCD /
    Farrar, Straus and Giroux, 2024.
Identifiers: LCCN 2023057426 | ISBN 9780374614058 (hardcover)
Subjects: LCSH: Afualo, Drew, 1995– | Internet personalities—
    United States—Biography. | Podcasters—United States—Biography. |
    Samoan Americans—Biography.
Classification: LCC PN4587.2.A38 A3 2024 | DDC 791.092—dc23/
    eng/20240226
LC record available at https://lccn.loc.gov/2023057426

Designed by Abby Kagan

Our books may be purchased in bulk for promotional, educational, or business
use. Please contact your local bookseller or the Macmillan Corporate and
Premium Sales Department at 1-800-221-7945, extension 5442, or by email at
MacmillanSpecialMarkets@macmillan.com.

www.auwabooks.com • www.mcdbooks.com • www.fsgbooks.com
Follow us on social media: @auwabooks, @mcdbooks, @fsgbooks

10   9   8   7   6   5   4   3   2   1

*This book is dedicated to my family, the love of my life,
and all of you.*
*All of whom made this book possible. I love you, thank
you; and fuck misogynistic men forever.*

If you talk to a man in a language he understands, that goes to his head. If you talk to him in his language, that goes to his heart.

—NELSON MANDELA

CONTENTS

LOUD

Heyyy, I'm Drew!

If you already know me, it's most likely from my TikTok, where I'm known as "Baba Yaga" to misogynists online. Or put another way, just like a heat-seeking missile, I target awful men who attack marginalized people on the internet for no reason and I never miss. Judging from their reactions, which range from bigoted attacks about my looks to actual death threats, I usually get the sense this is the first time these men have been taken to task for their comments. FYI, terrible men will degrade women and then fold like a lawn chair when I respond to them with silly-ass retorts like noting that they're "*built like a Lego*." That's on them. I want them to know there are consequences to treating people in ways that are harmful or problematic on a public platform, and so that's what I like to think of myself as: a tangible consequence.

I know you might be thinking: . . . *So?* How did a handful of short videos cackling right in the face of unfunny, misogynistic men lead to an audience of over nine million strong on socials, and the opportunity to write the book you currently hold in your hands?

It's because people, but especially women and femmes, are *tired*. *I* was tired. I was also mad seeing how life has forced women and femmes to center men even if it felt wrong and put us in uncomfortable or harmful positions. Like having to be cordial to a man who wouldn't leave me alone, because of the very real and valid fear that he might act violently toward me, all the way to being denied opportunities at work by a female supervisor because she had been taught to believe that there wasn't enough room for both of us in a space dominated by men. And when being mad no longer felt like enough . . . I decided to start laughing instead. Humor, I realized, was the gift I could share with every woman and femme out there who was over it just as much as I was.

If comparing these dudes' teeth to the doors of a haunted house could bring at the very least a snap of joy into someone's day, while possibly helping a few others question why these men have any say in how they feel about themselves, then I would gladly crack jokes all day long. My content found its audience in people who were *over* having to grin and bear men's bullshit, and the community I have built on my platforms has been a safe space ever since for everyone who is *tired* of holding space for misogynistic men. I don't just validate their experiences; I validate their anger. I tell them it's okay if you want to be mad, it's okay if you want to yell back, and it's okay if you want to be a bitch to men who are disrespectful to you or anyone around you. You have every right to feel the way that you do and express it in whatever way suits you best.

For every man who's had a meltdown after being faced with even 0.0001 percent of the shit that the rest of us have to face every day, there's someone like the woman who came up to me on a beach in Mexico with tears in her eyes to share that she was wearing a bathing suit for the first time in her life because of my content defending fat and plus-size women. Or the messages I've gotten from people telling me that I gave them the courage to finally report their assault. Or the woman in her fifties who left an abusive marriage after learning to assert herself from watching my videos. And I often think about the trans woman who told me that watching my battles against bigots online has kept her on this earth longer than she planned to be.

These kinds of stories inspire me to keep my foot on the metaphorical neck of misogynists online. If my dragging the assorted alpha males, gym bros, and hypermasculine podcast hosts of TikTok was what it took for my audience to find their voice, then I would be honored to take the wrath of millions of terrible men over and over again. Every single time.

Funny enough, all of this started with landing what I thought was my dream job.

I'd set my heart on working in sports entertainment ever since I was a kid watching my dad during his run with the Arizona Cardinals with my mom and big sister, Deison. As a proud Samoan, I found that professional football was the only stage I could reliably look to growing up for representation in the media (seriously, you can look it up—the Samoan community in America produces a remarkable number of professional football players per capita), and even then they were obviously only Samoan men. I wanted to grow up and *be* the representation I so desperately wished for—like a Samoan Michele Tafoya working as a sideline reporter on the field.

After I graduated from college with degrees in communications and sports journalism, it took two years of constantly applying for jobs and eight rounds of interviews for two separate roles before I finally landed the entry-level position that would get my foot in the door. In the spring of 2019, I was hired by the organization of my dreams as part of a grassroots initiative to boost female football fans' participation on their social media. Did the job include health insurance or any benefits? No. Was it technically classified as part-time though I had to sometimes come in five days a week and weekends, too? Yes. But did I care? No—I was convinced that all of this was part of the experience of being at the bottom of the corporate ladder, and I was willing, even eager, to pay my dues.

Landing this job was a monumental accomplishment for which I was so proud of myself. But after the initial rush of being hired wore off several months into the contract, I had to admit it wasn't going well. They almost never wanted to listen to, much less use, my ideas. The few that they did use always did well, but only my supervisor got credit for those. I was driving two and a half hours each way from my house to the company's headquarters for what was supposed to be my dream job, but I was miserable.

Ten months in, they announced that they were restructuring, which is just fancy corporate speak for "someone is about to get laid off." Which in this case was obviously me. I could not have been more heartbroken. As someone with borderline delusional confidence in everything I do (aka a Virgo), I had never considered the possibility that my dream job wouldn't work out. I'd pursued this goal longer than anything else in my life. The reality of it going down the drain so quickly and aggressively crushed my spirit in ways I had never anticipated. I know now that who I *am* and what I *do* should never be conflated, but at the time, I thought that failing to succeed in a system literally designed to be hostile to young women and especially young women of color somehow meant that I had failed as a person.

On the other hand, my family and my boyfriend, Pili, all of whom were self-employed and healthily skeptical of the company during my time there, were thrilled for me. Everyone was in agreement that this was a reason to celebrate. When I initially called my dad after it happened, he said, verbatim, "Congratulations!" My mom said, "This is the best thing that has ever happened to you." Although they empathized with me, none of them pitied me for even a second, because they were completely convinced that this failure would not define me. It wouldn't even leave a scratch. To be honest, I thought they were all out of their minds because, hello, I'd just lost my "dream" job—but it turns out they were completely right.

But first, the world shut down.

We all know what happened in the spring of 2020, when the coronavirus hit and we all had to be confined to our homes. With a newly depleted sense of self, I was extremely unsure of my future and what the hell I was supposed to do now—a feeling that had never been more foreign to me. I had never *not* known what I was going to do and how I was going to do it. I had no plan and no idea where to go from here. Also, living in quarantine under constant fear was an intensely unique brand of anxiety I think everyone was experiencing at once.

It was Pili who offered what no one could have predicted would be my way out. He suggested I make a TikTok account as a creative outlet to help cheer me up while we were at home. In those days, when I heard "TikTok," my brain immediately went to teenagers lip-syncing and dancing, essentially making me feel too geriatric to even exist on the app, let alone create content. But that all began to change during lockdown. Suddenly, everyone was on the app, including many creators that I started to love for their different niches and styles, and its new on-the-fly, quippy style of video content was surging in popularity as people searched for ways to connect.

Anyone who's used social media knows that there's no real way to manufacture virality. At first, I was just posting here and there, hoping that my friends and maybe a few other people would see the videos I was making on their For You pages. I talked about things that were important to me and that I could riff on, like a video about catcalling, or one showcasing the sweet things Pili would do for me as proof that we should all expect more from our male romantic partners.

And then it happened. One of my TikToks, a video about very specific red flags in men, blew up. I declared that any man who calls *The Wolf of Wall Street* his favorite movie of all time, or who has an obsession with Tom Brady—not the Bucs or the Pats, *just* Tom Brady—should be jailed (a clear and obvious joke, but also . . . is it?). And it went viral.

This was due in part to the onslaught of outraged men who flocked to my comment section and started stitching my videos to rally against me. But far more significantly, it was the result of an explosion in the rate of engagement on the post from other women, femmes, and nonbinary people who were fervently thanking me for articulating exactly what they had experienced, too.

The rest, as they say, is history.

To be honest, something I was wary about when I started writing this book was the memoir aspect of it. After all, I'm still in my twenties. I wasn't even certain I had lived a life interesting enough to warrant a memoir at all, let alone at this age. It's true that my life's changed in ways beyond what I could have ever imagined, but only in the last few years have I really started charting my own course.

Obviously, I have a lot of strong thoughts and feelings, and I am beyond honored when people who have found community within my platform reach out to me for advice, but I'm currently living my own life as well! That's not to say I don't always have something to say, because believe me I have no shortage of opinions (that's the Virgo in me). I just know there's literally no way for anyone to have all their shit figured out in their twenties—or possibly ever. No matter what happens to you, or when, you'll always continue to grow and evolve, and that's something to be grateful for.

But then I think about how, over the last few years, we've

built a fierce online community together supporting one another through the process of digging out the patriarchy that
has been deeply rooted in our brains. As much as my community loves to hear me roast terrible men on their behalf (and as
much as I enjoy doing it), the primary goal in what I do is
actually to *decenter* men. It is meant to empower you by taking *away* the power of misogynistic men when it comes to
how you value and see yourself. In a way, all of the videos I
post, the content I make, the men I drag, the people I uplift,
have been leading up to this moment. So in that regard, it's
fair to say this book is an extension of my videos, one that has
allowed me to dig deeper than ever before.

In case it somehow isn't already obvious, let me clarify up
front that this is definitely NOT a dating book. This is not
even a book about men, though it may seem like they feature
prominently. It's a book that focuses on internalized biases,
and how to uproot them from our lives—but most importantly it is a book about *you*, all the women, nonbinary, femme,
and queer people who I love, support, and will ride for, forever. And how truly life-changing showing up for one another
can be.

I can't share my boyfriend with you, but I am here to af-
firm that not only are you not asking for too much in a potential partner, but you should be asking for more. I can't share
my sister with you, but I can help you unpack any lingering
female rivalry so that you can experience true femme solidarity and friendship. I can't give you my self-confidence, but I
can help you realize how important it is to stand up for yourself. And I can't give you my cackle, but I can make you laugh,
and I plan to do so often along the way. So while I continue

to stay firmly planted on the necks of terrible men on the internet, this very text, through a combination of love, life lessons, and affirmative content, will be my guide and companion for you to work on the most important relationship of all: the one with yourself.

1

MEET THE AFUALOS

In September 1995, right at the tail end of Virgo season, my parents' dreams came true—and the prophecy of all the world's worst men came to pass: I was born.

I rolled into the world a nine-pound, twelve-ounce baby, and I like to think that I came out cackling. Not just because I'm Samoan and our people are known for their sense of humor, but because I was born knowing the best and funniest people in my life, still: my parents and my older sister. My parents named me Drew because my mom thought that a gender-neutral name would help me get job interviews later on in my life. She had seen a program on TV that explained how corporate businesses were more likely to choose the résumé of a man over a woman, after looking at the name, even if the qualifications were exactly the same. It's almost as if she knew that I would grow up to antagonize misogynists for a living, and my name would become one that would haunt terrible men, everywhere.

My immediate family consists of my parents, Deison, and my younger brother, Donovan, who was born when I was nine. We do have a really big extended family, first because Samoan families are *huge*, and also because my family has been in Southern California stretching back three to four generations. But when I was growing up, it was just the four of us (five, once Donovan was born) as a very tight-knit unit. It's why I consider my family members my best friends, support system, and confidants, because we've been close from the beginning.

As an aside, that's why I find it so funny when the anonymous misogynistic men in my comment section accuse me of "fatherless" behavior, because the reality is that I am entirely the way I am *because* my dad is so present and supportive. In addition to being a family-centric former athlete, he is a wonderful, caring, and emotionally intelligent person who has been a faithful and loving partner to my badass mom. Which, by the way, if you think *I'm* loud and outspoken, I know for a fact you haven't met my mom, who is both the breadwinner and the beating heart of our family.

My sister and I are two years apart in age but grew up going to school only one grade apart, and because my parents were pretty young when they had us, sometimes it felt like we all grew up together. Deison and I were surrounded by community, always. Our dad was often away because he was trying to parlay his college football success into a more steady and financially viable career. He started out as a walk-on in junior college (actually, a walk-by—he was just walking around campus and the coach asked him to join the team) and went all the way to the NFL. Still, I know everyone thinks professional athletes are rich, but the reality is that only a very small percentage earn the kind of money that makes headlines. And as this was going on our mom was launching her own career in corporate America and finishing school at the same time. We weren't financially well off, but we were rich in support. We had a cohort of extended and chosen family to help with our upbringing. I often say it was like I was being raised by the cast of *Friends* because the adults in my life were young and accessible. As they say, it takes a village to raise a child, and fortunately my siblings and I were no exception to that. This included my uncle and my godfather, who would take turns picking us up from school or taking us to sports practice or just generally stepping in and stepping up to make sure our childhood was as unaffected by any instability as possible. They were each instrumental in my upbringing, and are the reason I know that men today can do better, if they choose to do better: because I grew up witnessing it with my own two eyes.

On top of that, Deison and I had friends throughout middle and high school who'd get pseudo-adopted by our mom, living at our house for months on end. Seeing what a difference that kind of love from another family could make in people's lives, knowing they had a person who was completely there for them, no questions asked, made me so proud of my mom and so determined to be like her.

Because of this, or maybe because I trust them implicitly, I literally tell my parents *everything*. Not just the things that I think they would approve of, but also the hard, embarrassing shit. Because I know my mom will keep it real with me, and if I'm doing something she doesn't think I should do, she will tell me, point blank. And *usually* I will listen . . . but if I don't, she's only got herself to blame for my know-it-all mindset.

By Samoan standards, our immediate family is pretty small—just to give you a sense of what I mean, my dad comes from a family of five siblings, his dad from a family of nine, and his mom from a family of fourteen. My mom comes from a family of three, but her dad comes from a family of seven. And *his* dad remarried after my maternal great-grandma died, so at some point I gained a whole batch of step-cousins. Which makes it feels like I'm somehow always discovering a new cousin I never knew about.

Even though we're from a small island culture, we're loud and we're proud, and we'll *always* make sure you know you're in the presence of a Samoan—it's pretty easy; just follow the raucous laughter, because if there's anything my people know how to do, it's crack a joke. Nothing makes me prouder than when fellow Samoans reach out to me and tell me how much they see our culture—from my familiar cackle laugh to the jokes I make to drag sexist men by their half-court hairlines—embodied in everything I do.

To my fellow Samoans and Polynesians: It warms my heart that I can be some sort of representation for y'all. It truly is one of the best parts of what I do and not something I ever take lightly. My Samoan heritage is a torch I carry with so much love and thankfulness in my heart.

If there are three things the world knows about Samoans, they are: one, athleticism is in our bloodline; two, we love to celebrate; and three, we love to sing.

And when I say "celebrate," I mean that Samoans will celebrate life, death, and everything in between. Basically, we will find a reason to get together and we will sing, dance, eat, and drink. Funerals, birthdays, graduations, weddings, you name it: not only will we show up in droves, but we will bring enough food to feed a village (shout-out to my mom's potato crab salad, which is in such high demand that there was one year when we made it no fewer than six times in a weeklong span, for over two hundred people each time), and we will put on a production or floor show of some sort.

For example, graduations are a huge thing in Samoan culture, from both high school and college. Many members of your extended family will show up and cheer loudly and proudly. Afterward, we decorate you with hundreds of handmade candy and flower leis, and a handmade *kupuiga* or *haku* (which essentially is a celebratory headdress). It can be made of fresh flowers or money—either way, it's a statement.

Then, after the graduation, the graduate's family will host an *aiga*, or a party / family get-together—and when I say "party," I mean Party with a capital *P*. I'm talking literally hundreds of relatives, and friends. I loved going to these parties when I was a kid, because I'd get to see all my favorite cousins, and each time, it felt like a little reunion. Especially when I was younger and we'd be celebrating an older cousin's graduation, all the kids would get together after school three or four times a week to practice a coordinated dance in matching outfits that we'd then perform in front of our entire family at the *aiga*. After, we'd laugh, dance, sing, and eat all night.

Imagine doing that for *every* cousin. That was my childhood.

I didn't always feel super connected with my Samoan heritage when I was young, because I am not 100 percent Samoan (I have one white grandparent, out of four). But during events like these *aigas*, I'd feel so, so close to my culture. Seeing my extended family and community come together to put on an incredible celebration that would go on well into the night, complete with cultural dances like a traditional *siva* Samoa, a Hawaiian hula, a Maori haka, or a war chant dance that originated in New Zealand, and Tahitian dance, as well as enough food to feed everyone multiple times over and still have enough for leftovers . . . It would fill me with pride and joy. I would realize how lucky I was to be here, to be Samoan, to experience the overwhelming joy and energy of these celebrations that were unique to my culture.

As I mentioned before, Samoans celebrate every aspect of our existence: birth, life, and death. We honor those who come into this world, the milestones they achieve, and their passage into the next life. No joke, I've been to over thirty funerals, just because my extended family is so big and dedicated to celebration. We honor the living just as much as those who have passed on, because family is the most important thing in my culture.

I am going to take this space, because this is my book, to air a personal grievance about Samoans' love for singing. I find it almost disrespectful how every family gathering includes singing in some capacity, solely because I swear every Samoan is an amazing singer, EXCEPT ME. That Samoan gene seems to have skipped over me, and I take it personally to an extent. Which . . . whatever, that's cool, I'm definitely not salty about that at all. (I'm *bitter*.)

Samoan culture, at its genesis, is deeply matriarchal, which means strong women are celebrated, honored, and lifted up in many different ways. Just because my dad is six foot six and looks every inch the part of an "alpha male" doesn't mean he's the dominant one in my family. Not even close. My mom, all five foot three of her, has always been the head of the household and main breadwinner of the family.

Even though they have been together all my life, my parents didn't get married until I was four because my mom didn't want having children to be the main motivation behind getting married. She wanted to be sure that my dad was the one she could grow and evolve with, and she wanted him to be sure as well. She knew that a sense of obligation alone was a shaky foundation for a lasting family, and would be unfair to us as their children as well.

My mom has always been extremely ambitious and hardworking and, as a result, always stressed to her kids the importance of focusing on school above all. She worked hard enough that she was able to retire early, but I swear she's somehow more active now than she was when she was working three jobs and going to school. When I decided to pivot into a career in content creation, instead of questioning or discouraging me, my mom was all in, too, just as she's always been for anything I've been passionate to pursue. She's endlessly curious about how my new business works and how it grows, coming with me to strategy meetings and brainstorming sessions since becoming one of my managers. When I'm in a long period of traveling for my job, whether it's for media appearances, hosting opportunities, or partnership trips, the only thing I crave is the normalcy and steadiness of being home with my family.

My mom has an extremely strong personality and is very confident in herself and what she brings to the table, but it has never threatened my dad or made him feel like "less of a man." This is a really insidious accusation that I often find leveraged against women, and especially women of color. So many men are convinced that a woman in a heterosexual relationship who insists on being on equal footing with her male partner is asking for too much. Suddenly you're high maintenance, difficult, and overall an undesirable woman. Because if you, God forbid, start to think that you're actually EQUAL to men on an interpersonal level, you might start demanding respect in the workplace, media representation, and politics, too.

Which is ironic when we all know that the patriarchy makes it so that a heterosexual relationship will never be equal. Because, contrary to terrible men's belief, it's not that my dad merely tolerates or puts up with my mom running the show. Her strength, outspokenness, and confidence are exactly what draws my dad to my mom, and what makes him love, respect, and want to build a life with her forever. My mom makes my dad brave and gives him courage to try things. And my dad grounds my mom and reminds her that she deserves to rest and be taken care of, too. They inspire each other to want to be the best version of themselves, for the other, and that's something I've always strived for in my relationship. My parents are polar opposites in almost every conceivable way, but they are truly balanced with each other.

Simply put, my dad's pride and ego aren't wrapped up in harmful or otherwise limiting notions of how a man "should" be. He doesn't feel the pressure to be the breadwinner just because that's the role that is expected of men in a world ruled by patriarchy. While his nature isn't type A the same way my mom's is, he doesn't feel any kind of emasculation if he has to take on the majority of the household chores, or so-called typical women's work. In fact, he takes pride in assuming the domestic role, because it means that he gets to take care of the kids and the family and keep the house in order to support my mom's career, the same way she supported him when he was playing football. And because I was witness to my parents' incredibly equitable approach to parenting and domestic work when I was growing up, it helped me understand that there's no such thing as "lesser" work when it comes to building a family and being a good partner—it's all important.

Because I've been lucky enough to bear witness to my parents' deep love and respect for each other growing up, I've always known that I wasn't cut out to be put into a box of some shitty guy's expectations for what a wife "should" be, and that I'd literally rather die happy and alone than die unhappily partnered (more on this later). And the older I've gotten, the more my bullshit detector has been honed. To the point where if any man stepped to me with gendered expectations, like that I would be the one to make dinner on a night in when it hadn't been something that we'd discussed already or that I wouldn't dress a certain way, because I should not "want attention from other men," then I would tell them to get a dog, bitch. Because I don't adhere to a set of archaic gender roles or expectations at all, but especially if a man *requires* that of me. Prepare my grave for one girl; I'm dying alone, happily, instead.

Some people may say I'm being contrarian, but I say better to be contrarian than die a thousand little deaths of disrespect.

And you know what? I'm glad I held out, because the minute I fully embraced my zero-tolerance, *I'd rather die alone* policy, the universe sent me my soulmate, Pili. I knew that he was the one when I realized that our love for each other is rooted in the same level of trust that I witnessed in my parents' relationship. I'll talk more about Pili later, but the major thing that drew me to him was that for the first time, I felt like a man not only truly saw me for me, but loved every single part of me. Our love makes me feel free and like I finally know how to breathe for the first time in my life (yuck, being in love with a MAN is so bad for my brand, but whatever).

Even though Pili is tall and handsome and looks like a typical "alpha male," he has never needed to put me or the other women in his life down in order to feel strong. He has never, in all of our years together, complained that my success has made him feel "emasculated" (another word I believe to be a fallacy, because you can't feel "emasculated" if your self-validation doesn't come from overpowering your partner)—in fact, he's my biggest cheerleader and the reason I started posting content in the first place.

I want to take a moment here to unpack the concept of "women's work," which often refers to the invisible domestic labor that's done around the house—think cooking, cleaning, child-rearing, family schedule management, etc. Basically, all the shit that keeps a household running, aka project management at the absolute highest level. Which is why it makes me wanna scream when I think about how not only is "women's work" not monetarily compensated or even respected by our male counterparts, but it leads us to expect the impossible from modern women, who are supposed to have a full-time job AND be responsible for their kids' well-being AND cook a full dinner every night AND maintain a sense of beauty and youth that is not only unrealistic but exhausting.

I still remember the first time I saw the extent of this imbalance in person. As a young girl, I played soccer from the ages of seven to seventeen quite competitively. When you play at that level, especially when it requires traveling, the costs can really rack up. My dad would often barter services like fixing computers so that I could take lessons and afford to play. It also meant that 90 percent of the girls I was surrounded with came from much wealthier backgrounds than I did.

One of the girls I knew had a mom who was a high-powered lawyer and a dad who worked in property development. Her family had a housekeeper *and* a nanny, and yet when I went to her house for dinner, her mom was always in motion, cooking, cleaning, and making sure we were having a good time, while her dad just sat around. It's a memory that's always stuck with me because it was so incredibly different from anything I ever observed in my home, where my dad did the lion's share of the chores, and if he ever saw my mom struggling with something, he'd jump in to help unprompted, because it turns out most things go faster with two people instead of one.

It's not that I think her dad should've been the one cooking and cleaning instead, but that it would've made sense for the two of them to be working in tandem, as equals. And whether they said so explicitly or not, that kind of gendered dynamic sends a subliminal message to young people: *this* is what's expected from girls; *this* is what's expected from boys. It's how gender roles are internalized, and it's something that's always deeply frustrated me. Especially because at the *aigas* or other big Samoan family gatherings I attended when I was young, there was a very specific decorum we had to follow that was based on age and respect, not gender. Elders of the family were held in high esteem, and they were always served first. All kids, regardless of gender, were treated equally, and expected to help out equally—that meant cooking, serving, and cleaning up. The boys didn't think it was beneath them, and the girls never thought that it was their duty only.

But I still remember a dinner I went to years later in high school at a friend's house where, after a meal, all the women, including myself, immediately stood up to clear the table, and yet all the men stayed put, including my friend's brothers. The Samoan side of me urged me to keep helping out and being a good houseguest, but the feminist part of me hated that I was cleaning up after some entitled grown men I wasn't even related to.

On the flip side of that, I've found that even the most well-intentioned and "woke" men still never seem to understand what domestic labor equity actually looks like. Like the men who take out the trash twice a week and put the toilet seat down maybe every third time they pee and think . . . what? That they deserve a fucking medal for doing the absolute bare minimum? That they're better than the guy who jokes about how much he wishes his girlfriend would make him a sandwich? And in my opinion, at least the guy telling his girlfriend to make him a sandwich is unabashed and up front about his lack of respect for women. I don't know about you, but the only thing I hate more than a blatant misogynist is a misogynist who *swears* he isn't one. Because the latter means that he's not only a misogynist, but also a coward who won't admit it.

But the absolute worst are men who never seem to even recognize the efforts of their wives or girlfriends unless it serves them in some way, usually on social media. You know the type: on every Valentine's Day/birthday/anniversary/random Monday, he's finding a picture of him and his wife and writing a long-ass word-salad caption that calls her his "rock" and reveals that she does everything short of wiping his ass "uncomplainingly." He hits post and watches the likes roll in. He drones on and on about how incredibly selfless she is, no matter how many times he "messes up," she "always has his back." We all know this guy. We know this guy cheated multiple times. We know he's unemployed or "between jobs." And we know he consistently comments on his wife/girlfriend's weight, and cites that as the reason he's just "not as attracted" to her now, like he was back in the day. But most of all, we know he's a piece of shit . . . and she deserves better.

And that's how I know talk is fucking cheap. A social media post applauding your wife's cooking and cleaning skills is nothing more than a self-serving act. You really want to help? Then actually *help*. It's not unusual for Pili to do more around the house if I'm having a particularly busy workweek, or vice versa. It's just what makes sense because, as it turns out, human beings are capable of cooking and cleaning and however they identify doesn't affect their ability to do so (crazy, huh?).

Thanks to my Samoan upbringing, I was able to grow up relatively free from thinking of specific chores or tasks as "for" women or "for" men. Chores were done by whoever was able, capable, and around, and being a family unit meant we played to everyone's strengths for the collective well-being, not individual egos. My mom would always say, "We're all in the same boat, as a family. But it's a canoe and we all row in one direction; if someone is rowing against us, or not at all, they aren't being a team player in this family."

But even though my mom worked a lot when Deison and I were younger, she always made sure to be present in our lives and let us know that we were loved and that she was there. Family is everything to Samoans, and both my parents—my mom is half Samoan and my dad is full Samoan—have always stressed the importance of togetherness and tradition.

When I say that my mom is the beating heart of our family, I really mean it. When we were growing up, my mom made sure we never missed out on anything, whether that was school supplies, fun opportunities, family outings, or holidays. For example, we're a family of Disney lovers, and even though Disney has *never* been cheap, my mom always mysteriously found a way to surprise us with trips to Disneyland. She'd pull some strings, call in favors from a guy she knows, and the next thing you know, we're wearing Mickey Mouse ears in line for Space Mountain.

In fact, the running joke in my family is that my mom

always knows "a guy." As in, you need your car fixed for cheap? Mom knows a guy. You need to find out-of-season flowers? Mom knows a guy. You want to pull off something crazy for a birthday in two days and you have no idea where to start? Mom. Knows. A guy.

Every week, no matter how busy she was, we'd sit down to have what we call a "Family Fun Night," where we'd play board games and make sure to get in real quality time together as a family. She instilled in me the importance of cultivating that togetherness through special moments and celebration. Just like a flower grows through intentional care and attention, so does a family. My mom loves the holidays, especially Christmas, and I distinctly remember that when we were kids, she would individually wrap every single gift so that it always felt like we had more, even if the gifts themselves weren't expensive. Christmas is still a huge holiday for my parents, and my grandfather and my uncle always come celebrate it with us. But even when my mom goes all out with decorations and food, the only request she ever has, year after year, is that our entire immediate family takes a picture with Santa Claus at the mall. We've done this every year since Deison was born, and we will continue to do it for as long as we can.

Birthdays were just as special. When we were much younger, our mom, who was otherwise extremely strict about attendance, would let us skip school and take us to Disney (or whatever it was that we wanted to do for a day, but it was always Disney). As we got older and our birthday Disney trips moved to weekends, she'd wake us up with Starbucks and our favorite pastry with a candle in it, and have us open presents before school. As a result, to this day, gift giving is my top love language. My family eventually found financial stability as my dad moved back to California and my mom graduated and began moving up the corporate ladder, but I still treasure every moment of my childhood and have never found it lacking.

I am so grateful to my mom for showing me not only what true partnership looks like through the example of her relationship with my dad, but also what unconditional love looks like. I'm not suggesting that they were soft on us or spoiled us at all. On the contrary, my parents instilled in us from day one the importance of leading with kindness and respect for others and a drive to work hard at what we're passionate about, whatever that might be.

For my mom, that was making sure her family was always taken care of. She always put us first, and found genuine love and fulfillment in doing so. The moment that she received her first corporate bonus, instead of spending it on herself or even putting it away in savings, she spent it on sending Deison and me to see the Jonas Brothers in concert because she knew how much we loved them. And it wasn't just sending us to the concert, it was flying us out to Vegas, where they were playing, and even chartering us a damn limo to the venue, because she knew it'd create a memory that would last forever. She didn't grow up with that same kind of parental support, so she knew how important it is to show your kids you care about and support their interests, even if the interests are three random white boys jamming out onstage.

(Because when I say we loved them, let me stress just how much we LOVED them. I'm talking wall-to-wall Jonas Brothers magazine cutouts and merch in our rooms, hundreds of thousands of words of fan fiction, knowing EVERY single lyric by heart—you name it, we did it.)

Regardless of what she had to do to make it happen, she made sure that Deison and I never needed or wanted for anything growing up. When I compare our upbringing to my brother's, who was born when my parents were in a much different and better-off financial situation, I don't see any difference in the love, care, and attention we received. And even though my brother is both much younger and the only son of the family, my parents have never raised or treated him any differently than they did Deison and me. I don't talk about him as much, because he's still young and I don't want him to feel any pressure just because of my visibility, but I love him dearly and we are extremely close (I will fight him any day of the week, though—never forget that).

All in all, my mom is the coolest, most confident, and most hardworking person I know. She is 100 percent *that girl*.

Now—I want to talk about Deison. Where do I even begin?

I'll start off by saying that not everyone is as lucky to have a built-in best friend from the minute they were born. And I don't take our closeness for granted just because we're sisters or because we're similar, either, because I've met plenty of siblings who were raised the same but who turned out completely different. Not to say that Deison and I are exactly the same, but it's obvious when you talk to either of us for five minutes that we share the same two brain cells.

I think a lot of people who meet me first are a little surprised when they meet Deison, because they expect another version of me. But Deison and I are pretty different from the outside—she's five foot three, I'm six feet flat. She's a Sagittarius, and I'm a Virgo. She's gay, and I, unfortunately, remain attracted to men. She's also very soft-spoken and openhearted, which people would sometimes take advantage of when we were younger, whereas I'd be the first to tell you I'm a proud bitch, which meant that I've fought more people than I can count on her behalf (and other people's).

But Deison is also one of the only people I know who can go head-to-head with me and my sense of humor. She's kind, thoughtful, and generous in a way that inspires me to be a better friend and listener, because even I admit that I can let my contrariness and pettiness get the better of me. And though people might've thought Deison was a pushover when we were kids, she's actually one of my role models precisely because she lets her softness lead how she interacts with the world. When I'm at my most cynical, Deison reminds me to not just retreat into my shell but work harder to put out the energy I want to see in the world. And on the flip side, whenever I start getting truly out of pocket, Deison will be the first one to tell me I'm acting like a clown. Deison makes me a better person, and in return, I'll beat the ass of anyone who tries to bully or be mean to her.

Pretty fair trade, I'd say.

My life now is nothing like what I thought it would be when I was younger—it's beyond my wildest imagination, and I am just so stoked and grateful for all the opportunities my journey has allowed me. But I also know that forging a career out of social media and content creation, as I'm doing, is a great unknown, simply because this industry is so new, and there's no accounting for what might come next. Honestly, if you told me tomorrow that I'd lose all of my audience and no one would know who I am anymore besides my family and friends, I'd be fine with it. If through my content I've helped even one person gain more confidence and empowered them to leave a shitty situation they were in—which I believe I have, based on the testimonies I've received from so many of you—then I'm satisfied. And because I know that I have an incredible family and support system around me who have always held me down and empowered *me* to be the woman I am today.

Whenever I travel for work, I bring along, at minimum, my boyfriend, Pili, my mom, and Deison, as well as my hair and makeup artist, Adam, who in addition to being *THAT* bitch, *period*, also happens to be my cousin. If I can swing it and there's the opportunity to extend a work trip into a longer family trip, I'll also bring along my dad and Donovan (as long as it doesn't interfere with school). If I have an opportunity to share all the new things I'm experiencing with my favorite people in the world, why wouldn't I take it?

You can't choose your family, and I know I'm extraordinarily lucky to have the one that I do, but you can choose the people who are around you. Even now, when I choose partners to work with, whether that's on my management team or brands who pitch me ideas, I look for the same qualities that my mom instilled in me so long ago: people who lead with respect and kindness, who are driven by passion, and who find making bigoted men cry just as hilarious as I do.

2

BE YOURSELF, AND OTHER IMPOSSIBLE BUT NECESSARY LIFE LESSONS

I **know some,** if not most, of y'all are probably here for jokes, of which I promise there are plenty, but I also want you to know that I do not take this subject lightly. When I look back at my early twenties, my teenage years, and my adolescence, I realize I *have* been through some shit. I might not have always responded in a way that was proper, but I am proud of how much I've grown and how far I've come. As nerve-wracking as the future can be for someone like myself, a few things I am confident in are my morals, my values, and knowing with crystal clarity what matters most to me in this world. I may not have it all figured out, but the me of today is someone I'm proud and happy to be, and the me of tomorrow is someone I am excited to become. I hope that sharing my experiences will save you from making life-changing mistakes, or even offer some sort of comfort as you navigate yours.

All this is to say that one of the most beautiful, and scariest, things about growing up is growing into yourself. I'm not talking about the surface-level stuff, like how you dress or what your aesthetic is or how you do your nails or present yourself on social media. Obviously, all that is part of it—it's literally my entire career—and it's especially important for anyone who exists outside of Western beauty standards or the gender binary to have an outlet of expression and see depictions of themselves outside of traditional media channels, but what I've always been more interested in are the less tangible qualities. What you value, what you stand for, what you live for. Who you really *are* and how you want to be seen.

As someone who has a younger sibling and younger cousins, and has interacted with countless young people through my platform, I know the question of *Who am I?* can be one of the toughest things to figure out. I think what's just as important, if not more important, is *Who do I want to be?* because it's pretty hard to know where you'll end up if you don't know where you currently are. That's part of what I'm hoping this book will help you explore: learning who you are is one of the hardest things to achieve, so if at any point this book gives you a moment of epiphany or solitude in which you feel like you've come closer to understanding yourself, then I'll feel like I've succeeded.

One of the foundations of human psychology is the concept of self-awareness, which is the ability to identify yourself, contextualize yourself in the environment you exist in, and understand your own thoughts, feelings, desires, and boundaries. From a psychological standpoint, most children will have started developing self-awareness by the age of five, which for me, at least, is around the age from when I can actually re-member liking things, like my favorite color at the time, my first friends outside of my sister, my favorite playground activ-ities, my favorite toys, etc. In hindsight, it was the start of me beginning to understand myself.

Something I'm ever grateful to my parents for in how they raised me and my siblings is that I was lucky enough to have freedom from so many of the shackles of patriarchy that would cause fear, anxiety, and insecurity later on (relatively, anyway. Unfortunately, we are never fully immune to the effects of the patriarchy).

Not only did they take us seriously as developing young people, but they encouraged our interests, no matter how fa-natic or silly. Discovering new things to love is fun, and it's a kind of joy I appreciate more and more the older I get. Just think back to when you were young and you listened to or experienced something for the first time and had the magical feeling that you'd discovered something that felt tailor made for you. Like the first time I watched a Jonas Brothers music video or the first time I went to Disneyland and knew imme-diately that I'd found something I was going to love forever (my hunch was wrong about Nick Jonas, but I was definitely right about my love for Disney). The older you get, the rarer it is to have that feeling. Part of it is that there is a lower likeli-hood of discovering something for the first time, the same way everything to a child is new and fresh. Regardless, the older I've gotten, the more I try to intentionally carry that sense of discovery and wonder with me whenever possible. I consider it a twofold lesson: one, not to default to cynicism or nihilism; and two, to let it lead me to actively seek out new experiences. I think it's important to keep this sense of wonder and adoration of the world to really remain grounded in the present.

There are other things, too, like asserting your boundaries and vocalizing your needs, which, as a child, could be something as simple as refusing to eat a food you don't like or to participate in an activity you don't want to. Kids let you know what they want as soon as possible, with zero hesitation. Obviously, it gets more complicated as you get older, and situations aren't nearly as easy to navigate, and I'm definitely not advocating that anyone throw tantrums just to get their way, but I do know this: it is extremely important to hold on to that fearless assertiveness from childhood, which, unfortunately for women and femmes, is something that we're socialized out of as we grow up—and that I am currently paying my therapist to help me relearn.

Paradoxically, the more we're able to know, understand, and *be* ourselves, the more we also realize how difficult it is to do so. That's self-awareness, too, baby.

And that's not even including highly specific generational experiences, like how millennials came of age with the internet and the invention of blogging and social media and Gen Z came of age during a time of global pandemic and social isolation just as developments in social media and technology were creating new ways to curate ourselves. As a millennial born right on the cusp, I feel like I was just old enough to observe the shift happening in how we understand and position ourselves in the world even as I was actively living through it.

So if childhood is this rich and ripe time for self-development, what goes on as you get older? Why is it that so many people, not just women and femmes, experience insecurity or anxiety, and seem to get waylaid on the journey to finding themselves?

Well, as the French philosopher Jean-Paul Sartre famously said, "Hell is other people."

As you grow up, those early years of developing self-awareness are suddenly put on warp speed, and the number of things that you are exposed to increase exponentially. There are a million new things to react to, and so many new perspectives to consider. And an important, but difficult, skill to develop is knowing which of those perspectives are coming from people who have your best interests at heart and which are coming from people who are judging you. The world that might have at one point seemed manageable and self-contained is suddenly expanded to include new schoolmates, teachers, friends of friends, and, for those of us who grew up on the internet, countless strangers online. Along with the increasing awareness of the tensions consistently growing within the pressure cooker of a patriarchal society, there is relentless messaging from all around us, growing louder and louder, that there's a specific way to act in order to be accepted, whether that's from family, movies and TV shows, books, toys, social media, or any number of things that go into making up a person's worldview, and start to greatly affect it.

Even with my rock-solid family foundation, this was true for me when I started to realize that I was entering a phase of my life when what I wore, how I talked, how I acted, and even who I liked or hung out with were all up for judgment, and that I would never again be able to return to the days of carefree childhood ignorance. Having that realization is a scary moment in itself. This period of burgeoning selfhood is when our self-perception and values are evolving and most in flux, and it can be difficult to navigate.

As confident as I am in myself now, I haven't always been that way. And this can be especially difficult as a femme of color, or if you're queer or questioning your identity in any way, because as hard as it is to come of age within societal norms, it's even harder outside of them.

I think (hope!) it's normal to look back on your early teen years and cringe a little. I'd be disappointed in myself if I didn't. But recently I've started having more patience for teenage Drew. Yes, maybe now I have to deal with bills and taxes and sad, awful men who have nothing better to do than get their feelings hurt by me online, but teenage Drew had her hands full with everything from being head and shoulders taller than everyone in her eighth-grade class, to protecting her sister from people taking advantage of her kindness, to figuring out who the hell she was. From something as serious as dealing with racialized and sexualized bias from strangers and classmates alike, to something as juvenile as a childhood crush.

I'd like to take a moment to reflect on crushes, which are such a big part of being a young woman, whether you had your own crushes or were just a witness to other people's crushes, as I mostly was. The crazy thing about crushes developed at that specific age on the edge of girlhood and becoming a teenager is how they can make you literally feel like you're dying when you have one, and then one week later, when the crush clears, you suddenly have no idea what you were even drawn to in the first place. Everything else at that age is so chaotic, it makes sense that romantic experiences would be, too. But there's also something so precious about childhood crushes, as these are often our first gateways into understanding something new about ourselves.

Deison had tons of crushes growing up. I was the opposite. What can I say? I developed a disdain for men early on . . . and, yes, I'm a Virgo who needs to be in control of her emotions and actions at all times (and maybe this isn't related to astrology at all, but I just love to blame things I can't explain about my personality on the stars). If I ever *did* show interest in men, they were celebrities, and I don't know if it was a conscious choice, because I knew celebrities weren't real the same way my male classmates were, or because of my low-key delusions of grandeur. Because even at a young, impressionable age, I always believed that I was destined for greatness, both professionally and romantically. I like to think my standards have been high since I could even begin to conceptualize romantic relationships, and that's how I want all of you to think.

At the same time, crushes are fun. The hours I spent with my sister and our friends writing Jonas Brothers fan fiction or analyzing every frame of their music videos are among some of my favorite childhood memories. Especially at that age, I'd argue that crushes are particularly important outlets of energy for preteen and teenage girls, who are blithely unaware of a life that does not revolve around frivolous pursuits, like crushes on men who may or may not deserve attention. And crushes, especially on fictional characters or celebrities, united us with friends and other fans in a community to safely and jointly explore what we wanted and navigate how we interacted with the world.

But around the time we were in late middle school and early high school, my friends and classmates began to move from the fantasy realm for crushes into reality. That is to say, they began frequently pursuing relationships with, or at least having crushes on, real-life boys almost exclusively. In the most extreme cases, they were *getting boyfriends.*

Neither Deison nor I dated in high school. It was something my mom actively discouraged because she wanted us to focus on school. I've had the mindset of a forty-five-year-old man since I was ten, so this wasn't an issue with me, but I was very protective of Deison, someone who did have many crushes on inferior men (and she turned out to be gay, so go figure). I was suspicious of anyone who could hurt her, so we both approached these new developments warily. As our friends started to adapt to this new ecosystem of dating and we all entered this world of male validation, I began to wonder if there was something wrong with my perspective. It was fine to think about going on dates in the abstract, but with the subpar men in our school? I couldn't understand it. Anything beyond that was beyond me, and yet it was an energy that seemed to be taking over all of my and Deison's friends during those late middle school and high school years.

I wasn't the only one who took notice of the changes in the people around me. My mom, who started a family with her high school sweetheart (though she made him wait nearly a decade to prove himself a worthy life partner, even after they had two kids together), was no stranger to the possibility of first love. And if we'd really found a person we wanted to be with, she would've been the first to support us. But I think she knew that it's easy to fall prey to male validation at that age, and she wanted to stress the importance of our self-worth and confidence outside of that ideology. That's something I'm extremely grateful for, especially looking back on my journey and understanding how that led me to where I am now.

Our parents never strictly prohibited us from dating, since they knew that would be impossible, nor did our dad fall into the toxic masculinity cliché of trying to "protect" his daughters by treating us like property or threatening violence on anyone who came near us. He just wanted to make sure that we understood his ultimate priority was our physical safety. It was my mom who spearheaded the parental approach when it came to our budding love lives. She knew exactly how to talk to us to make sure that we knew we could have all the crushes we wanted—we just had to learn to be very careful when it came to acting on them.

She told us, "If I find out that one of you is dating and the other one didn't tell me, well, first, just know that I *will* find out. And when I find out, you're *both* getting in trouble for not telling me." And the thing is, my mom really would've found out. Moms know everything, but especially mine. When she sat us down and told us that, Deison and I looked at each other and we knew that we'd be keeping each other in check and that there was no way in hell we'd let the other person get a boyfriend.

So did my mom kind of evil mastermind the entire situation and play to our protectiveness for each other so we'd do her dirty work for her? I'm not sure. She is a genius, though, so I wouldn't be surprised.

My parents clearly didn't have that much to worry about anyway, given that Deison likes women and I can barely tolerate most men now, but by not expressly forbidding us from dating, they instead did something that was pretty transformative, especially for two girls at that age: They gave us the power to choose. They created a situation that made the two of us expressly aware that every choice you make doesn't just affect yourself but also the people around you, and that every choice has consequences. So, sure, we *could* date—we just had to be willing to accept the consequences that came with dating.

Instead of creating strict rules for what we could and could not do, our parents instead set forth guidelines that did not set out to curtail the impossible while still creating safeguards so that we wouldn't lose focus on the things we wanted to do in life, of which having an unserious relationship at fourteen was probably not one. And because these guidelines were in line with the values that they'd raised us with, we were more than happy to respect them, especially because I felt like my parents took me and my interests seriously in other ways.

The older I get and the more I hear I'm like an older sister to y'all, the more I realize how hard being an older sister/parental/mentor figure is, and how good my parents were at it. But especially now that I'm the age they were when they were raising us, I have a newfound appreciation for them and hope to emulate them in my interactions with younger friends and fans. Because you see how much someone trusts and respects you, and you want to live up to that. You also want to reciprocate that sentiment, which means placing your trust in someone you're also meant to be guiding. You know how hard it is for a know-it-all like me to keep it to myself when I see someone doing something I would never do? Damn near impossible. But sometimes being a parent or a mentor or a teacher means letting someone make their own choices (within reason, obviously) while quietly making sure that you're there to support them if it doesn't turn out the way they want or expect.

My father always said about how he raised us, "If I open the door to trust, then I have to actually trust them." The greatest gift you can give anyone, but especially a young person, is trust. Because if you show someone that you trust that they can make their own decisions, they in turn will trust you enough to come to you when they need someone if it turned out to be a life lesson. I always knew I could come to my parents, even with my mistakes, because I knew I could trust that they would not only be there, but also be there without judgment.

Although my sister and I didn't date in high school, I was still fascinated by my friends who were exploring their first relationships, even if I personally hadn't found someone I wanted to explore that with. After all, first relationships and first loves are important milestones, ones that I still wanted to experience.

But the more I heard about boyfriends and sex from friends, the more confusing it got. Because even at that age, I could recognize that the tendencies my friends were describing from these immature boys were nothing short of fuckboy behavior—and mind you, this was long before I even knew what fuckboys were. But if that's what all the movies and TV shows told me to want, and it's what all my friends seemed to want, it made sense that I would want it, too, at some point . . . right?

After all, these were the years when we were experiencing peak gender socialization. By that I mean everything from the draconian dress code at my school, which didn't allow girls to wear anything that didn't pass the "fingertip rule," to the complicated social dynamics of middle and high school, where girls were expected to be smart but not too smart (or you're a know-it-all), and friendly but not too friendly (or you're a slut). Which, as a result, would lead to stereotypes or unwritten rules like *Girls are drama.* Or *If you show your feelings, you're not a real man.* Or *Any girl who talks to more than one guy at a time is easy.* Later in this book, I want to take the time to unpack how we even arrived at these misogynistic myths. But back then, these were such widely held beliefs that as a teenager I blindly accepted them as truth, even if now just typing out those words makes me feel sick. And that's how the patriarchy functions: by creating arbitrary rules meant to punish women and brainwashing women into not only believing them, but upholding them, too.

It all creates an environment where teenage boys can get away with insensitive and hurtful behavior and have it waved away as *boys will be boys*, or even to have that kind of behavior somehow make them more attractive in the high school dating field and beyond. It's why the patriarchy is such a trap, because falling into it will do nothing but reinforce harmful beliefs that have women pushing other women down to further uplift men. And it's crazy because the deeper we fall into this mindset at a young age, the longer we spend in it, and the more difficult it is to undo it later on. It's how the patriarchy continues to sustain and claim more foot soldiers, no matter how adamant we are about wanting to unlearn it.

I'm embarrassed to admit it, but I definitely bought into this mentality when I was younger, which is what led me to being a pick-me girl in high school, aka catering fully to male attention and approval (more on this dark period of my life later). And it wasn't until much later that I gained the clarity to question how fucked up this prioritization of male ego is, and I was finally able to reflect on just how insidious our male-dominated culture really is, and how young it starts. I mean, damn, it starts even before birth, with gender reveal parties and baby registries. Who decided that only boys can like trains, trucks, and Legos and only girls can like dolls, bunnies, and Easy-Bake Ovens? How many times have I heard someone try to get their son to stop crying by telling him that boys don't cry? Why do we tell boys as young as five or six that hobbies like drawing or playing house are girly, or tell girls that being too dominant at certain sports can be emasculating to young men? Why are so many school dress codes, even in elementary school or middle school, clearly targeted toward policing women and their bodies?

The good news is that most people (operative word: "most") eventually come to recognize how casually sexist these beliefs are. They start to see the harm in perpetuating an ideology that pits women against one another and props them up in a way that values them as nothing more than accessories in the lives of men. The bad news is that, like the flu virus, these rules and beliefs seem to mutate over the years as each successive generation deals with its own version of these gendered stereotypes and expectations, and it doesn't feel like it'll end anytime soon. It constantly evades eradication, by adapting to new environments and growing stronger through each "mutation." I'm thinking, for example, of the early feminist focus on women's right to work, and once that was achieved, the realization that women were paid, promoted, and hired less, which is an ongoing concern. Even as we move extremely slowly toward addressing the gender gap, there's now an expectation that not only will women hold down a full-time job, but they're also meant to be the primary homemakers and family caretakers. We expect women to be everything and take on more and more of the burden, while our expectations for men stay exactly where they are. Tell me, where's the equality in that?

As difficult and commendable as it is to recognize just how damaging these thought patterns are, it's even more difficult to unlearn them. It remains a journey, even for me. Knowing that is why I always center the effort and willingness to learn, and *truly* learn, not just co-opt the language and do none of the work. Men who think they deserve recognition for self-identifying as feminists but also act like that's where the journey ends can miss me with that fake solidarity bullshit.

This is why the people you surround yourself with are so important, because they can provide context and a trusted sounding board for how to navigate this scary new world. Looking back at the teen I was then and the self-assured adult I am now, I know I owe it to my parents and older family members and friends for guiding and uplifting me. Now that

I'm in the position that they were in, it's my duty to pass on the mentorship that they gave me, which is why I'm so determined to empower young women and femmes in particular.

What I find especially heinous is when this kind of prejudiced socialization comes from ignorant adults who don't understand the weight that being in a position of power over others carries. For example, when I was in middle school, there was a semester when my grades in math class plummeted. I had always been a conscientious student, raised by my parents to take school seriously and work hard in all of my classes. My mom didn't understand how I was suddenly failing a subject I had gotten straight As in up until that point. But it was because that year, I had been placed in a class with a teacher who was so disparaging and so cruel that I became frozen with fear in her classroom, to the point that I refused to raise my hand and dreaded having to go to her class. And it wasn't just me—this teacher had a pattern of making *all* the nonwhite students in her class uncomfortable. In retrospect, I can name her clear racial bias for what it is, but at the time, all I knew was that just the thought of going to her class filled me with such trepidation that it was sapping my energy and affecting not only my grades but also my self-esteem.

In a Samoan family, teachers and other figures of professional authority are held in especially high regard because of their role in the community, imparting knowledge and shaping the minds of young children. At twelve, I still believed that because she was a teacher, she deserved my respect. I was lucky to have perceptive parents who I trusted enough to share my honest feelings. Once I shared my experiences in this teacher's class with my mom, she immediately saw this teacher's behavior for what it was and raised hell with the school administration. She didn't leave any doubt that what was happening was unacceptable.

That this person was not only a full-grown adult but one who had been entrusted with the education of young people is chilling when I think about the long-term effects of this behavior gone unchecked. People like her pass on their own misguided beliefs to malleable young people, whether it's intentional or not, which then elicits a new kind of violent prejudiced dynamic as it evolves with each new generation.

No one is born with sexist and racist beliefs—the idea that a group of people might be superior to others based on gender or race is a man-made construction, and a core part of Western colonialism and patriarchy. Hateful people beget hateful people, so if I meet a young person who has deep-seated sexist and racist beliefs, I know it's because there was a series of adults in their life who really let them down. And so it is the responsibility of anyone who is a parental figure, teacher, or mentor to make sure they are proactively shaping the points of view of the young people in their lives without bias.

But there is also a time in everyone's life when it is no longer enough to passively let these biases shape us. At some point, it does become our duty to seek out information, educate ourselves, surround ourselves with different perspectives, and decide if we're going to let the status quo stand or do the hard work of pushing back against it. There are many factors working against marginalized people when it comes to letting these toxic mindsets go, what with our forced assimilation in a racist/sexist/homophobic/transphobic world, especially when those prejudiced beliefs are ingrained in our minds far before we can identify them. It's not our fault if we are born ignorant, but it is our fault if we die that way.

The older we get, the more we become attuned to the world's expectations, both good and bad. Believe me, I know how difficult it can be to question or resist something that is embedded in the very fabric of our society. It has cost me everything from male friends who aren't comfortable being questioned on their chauvinist beliefs, to literal money lost from business opportunities. To those cowards, I say: GOOD RIDDANCE. That reaction is exactly *why* I have dedicated myself to being as loud and annoying about calling out and calling attention to injustice on any level and at any scale as soon as I see it, so that no one is ever left second-guessing or internalizing these macro- or microaggressions.

The complicated question of identifying who we are, who we will become, and *how* to become that person isn't one that can be answered by anyone but ourselves, but what I hope for all young people reading this is that you are allowed the fullest opportunity to explore that question, no matter what that journey looks like, and that in your rush to grow up, you never forget the child you once were—the beautiful thing about being alive is that there is something valuable to be learned at every phase of it.

3

CONFESSIONS OF A TEENAGE PICK-ME

People love to accuse me of being "too hard on men." They love to say, "but not all men!" And by "people," I mean bigoted people, or bigot sympathizers . . . which makes their opinion automatically invalid to me. Their opinion doesn't mean anything to me for multiple reasons we'll get into, but the reality is that, no matter how great a man can be on an individual basis, all men benefit from the patriarchy. So yes, that includes men you love and admire, and even the men in my own life, like my brother, my dad, or Pili. I'm not pulling any punches even when it comes to them, but especially when it comes to you.

The world is literally set up to provide cis men with un-limited chances, and I'm just not interested in contributing to that. Instead, I make it my life's mission to extend that energy and generosity to women and femmes, who I will support and ride for until my last breath. But the funny—or maybe fucked-up—thing is that women are often men's biggest defenders. As much positive feedback as I've gotten from people who feel empowered by my content, I've gotten nearly as much criticism from people in my comments trying to "not all men" me. What really disheartens me is when it's women doing that. They try to tell me that I've gotten it all wrong, that even though the men I fuck up online are willfully bigoted on the internet, I still "went too far." These men don't even meet the basic minimum of human respect for other people, and yet some women feel the need to defend the entire male gender in my comment section.

To those women, first of all, I want you to dig deep down and examine just why my videos are setting you off the way they are. Respectfully, it's not even about you, so why do you feel the need to respond? Did I call out your boyfriend/fiancé/husband by name? No? Then why do you feel so personally attacked? Why do you feel the need to take up this mantle for a man you don't even know? A man who, in his own words, has expressed an extreme distaste for women? Have you considered the fact that this may be something you need to address within yourself or directly with your boyfriend/fiancé/husband, and not me, a total stranger on the internet?

But unless a woman is outright hateful and abusive to others, I don't believe in using my platform to shame or call them out the same way I call out terrible men, because I know that if they're in my comments trying to defend an awful and mediocre man they don't even know, they're, unfortunately, still in their pick-me era.

If you don't know what a pick-me is, just think about the phrase. Imagine a group of women standing before some (most definitely undeserving) man, all begging him to notice them, to choose them, to pick them. I'm unsure of the terminology's exact origins, but I believe it comes from the climactic scene in *Grey's Anatomy* where Meredith Grey is begging Derek Shepherd to "pick me" instead of another woman. Y'all remember the scene, right? "Pick ME, choose ME, love ME" . . . The sentiment is both literal and metaphorical. One woman leveraging her self-worth in exchange for a man's affection, all at the expense of another woman. This might mean engaging in "not like other girls" behavior, like shunning or disparaging interests or hobbies more commonly held by women and femmes or exaggerating or pretending to have an interest in certain things that are more appealing to men in order to be "one of the boys." Or it might mean allowing certain disrespectful behavior to slide just to show how "cool" and "chill" you are.

Just think about the "cool girl" monologue from the movie/book *Gone Girl*, delivered by the antiheroine Amy Dunne, who fakes her own murder and frames her husband when she discovers he's been cheating on her even after she uprooted her life to move to his hometown in Missouri with him. As Amy describes her, the "cool girl" adores sports, poker, dirty jokes, and burping, plays video games, and drinks cheap beer. Is understanding. *Never* gets angry. Just smiles in a chagrined, loving manner and lets men do *whatever* they want. To me, though, the most striking part of this monologue is the moment when she reveals the "cool girl" for the sham that it is: *Men actually think this girl exists. Maybe they're fooled because so many women are willing to pretend to be this girl.*

Unfortunately, women *are* willing to pretend to be this girl, because when you're brainwashed by the patriarchy, being "cool" is the greatest compliment you can receive from a man. It's almost regarded as a badge of honor, or a crumb of validation we're meant to not only live off of, but continue to chase. Because that one word implies everything a girl "shouldn't" be: jealous (just because she wants assurance from her partner), demanding (just because she doesn't let her partner always prioritize hangouts with "the boys" over doing housework or spending time as a couple), hysterical (just because she's rightfully angry about discovering that he's been sliding into other girls' DMs)—aka, you know, just logical reactions. But then again, the very definition of misogyny is that men don't see women as deserving bare-minimum respect.

The first time I watched this movie, I was nineteen, and never had I felt so personally seen while hearing words that put so much of the world around me into perspective, because sadly, seeking male validation is something *all* women and femmes have suffered from at one point or another in their lives, myself included. Having that realization really triggered a flashback to some of my memories. How many times had I let male behavior slide in order not to kick up a fuss or seem difficult? And for what? A fleeting acknowledgment of chillness by a man with an underdeveloped frontal cortex? If that's what being a "cool girl" gets you, then you know what? Fuck being cool and fuck being chill. If the reward for being the "coolest" girl in the room is a sliver of attention from the world's most mediocre men, then I would happily commit to never being chill. And never being cool. But maybe the "cool girls" got one thing right after all: I wouldn't be like the other girls—I was going to be much, much worse.

Of course, there are plenty of women and femmes who do enjoy football, dirty jokes, burping, and cheap beer. I, personally, am fond of a few of them. The difference between teenage Drew and the Drew of today, though, is that I no longer think my interest in those things makes me special or different, nor do I want it to. I no longer give two shits if the things I like make me more or less appealing to men.

Because that is the essence of a pick-me, someone whose life is so geared toward male approval that it colors everything she does. That desire for male approval is what underwrites a pick-me's belief that somehow no other woman likes a specific thing, say, the NFL, the same way she does, with the same expertise or knowledge, and so she can *only* legitimately discuss it with men. So it follows: if she is the only woman who can "relate" to men and/or discuss this interest with them, then she is more likely to be "picked" by men. The reductive math is quite simple.

Or think about the pick-me's claim that she's totally fine with how much her boyfriend salivates over Instagram models or flirts with his coworker, because *she's* not like other girls who are jealous and insecure. But I'm here to tell you that having boundaries like this crossed by your monogamous partner is not something that you should have to normalize just to appease a man's fantasies, and it doesn't inherently make you insecure to care about holding those boundaries. The problem with this cavalier and misogynistic attitude is that not only is it delusional and dishonest, it's a race to the bottom. If your approach to connecting with anyone, not just men, is based on superiority, then it will never provide a stable foundation for a meaningful relationship of any kind.

Pick-mes do not just operate in the interpersonal arena, but in professional spaces as well. I've been in many rooms where I've been the only woman and/or the only person of color, and it has never made me feel empowered or like a winner, just isolated and ignored. I can't understand why anyone, but especially women/femmes who grow up in a patriarchy and watch the violence it inflicts on them, would subscribe to that isolating and lonely ideology.

I want to clarify before I go on, so that people don't misunderstand. Although I don't have any patience for the pick-me girl, I do have empathy for her. How could I not? Not only do I understand her, I *was* her. Even though I've always been outspoken, for almost my entire adolescence, from the start of middle school to my early college years, I craved male approval. It wasn't a conscious decision, but it was an inevitable one. The experience of being indoctrinated into a misogynistic perspective when they are born into a patriarchy is one that is not exclusive to me. Looking back, I see how, for years, I would do things like prioritize men's feelings over my own comfort or safety, or buy into the idea that receiving male attention somehow made me special. These were often men I didn't even really know, much less like or respect, so the fact that I was letting their opinion rule my life and my self-esteem is ludicrous in retrospect.

So how can I not feel sorry for the pick-me? She is living a life devoid of color and unconditional love and support from women. Because just like I realized when I was younger, that is what life becomes when you gear it toward men: empty.

As a former pick-me myself, I can spot all the signs from a mile away, and I know the importance of understanding the nuance of holding space for those women/femmes who are still lost, while also understanding that it isn't our job to save everyone. You can't save people who don't want to be saved. But I do also believe that the minute they're able to correct their mindset and undo their pick-me behavior, they're going to realize that life is *so* much better on the other side. They'll see, once and for all, that living your life according to the whims of men is no way to live.

I also understand that women are socialized to engage in this behavior, because as many developments as we've had in women's liberation and the wide embrace of feminism, it is undeniable that modern society was created by men, and prioritizes their dominance at the expense of everyone else. Being a pick-me is the defense mechanism women develop in response when we understand, whether implicitly or explicitly, that the playing field has never been, is not, and may never be, level. After all, men are paid more and promoted faster and more often. Men sit at the heads of the overwhelming majority of the world's media companies, universities, and cultural institutions, and are taken more seriously by employers, doctors, and teachers. As if that weren't bad enough, it pits women against one another as well. The ideology convinces us that there can only ever be *one* woman who can be noticed and gifted with attention from men. And if you were to factor in industries that are male-dominated on top of that? Any chance of solidarity among women, especially in the workplace, is obliterated. And regardless of the vast improvements that have been made by way of female empowerment in the last century, the truth is that power is still concentrated in the hands of cis, straight, white men.

And so, faced with how daunting a realization that is, women realize that our gender expression makes us vulnerable to harm, discrimination, and violence, which also leads us to anticipate it. That, in turn, triggers the biological impulse that compels us to seek safety. And the greatest myth that any dominant structure tells the people it's oppressing is that through suppressing or disparaging others like ourselves, we can convince those in power that we are not only worthy of protection but somehow *more* worthy than others. This is the competitive environment that brings out the pick-me in people, but where the only people who come out on top are those who had power all along. It's nothing more than a distraction to turn us against ourselves, because if we're focused on one another, we won't notice misogynistic men closing (and holding) the door behind them. The contradictory nature of a pick-me is that it sets up a dynamic where you will *never* be equal if you have to ask for it in the first place.

A perfect example of this is an experience I had after my

platform had been established. An awful man made a violently bigoted video about me, spurring on the never-ending song of involuntarily celibate men calling me unoriginal names like "fat" and "ugly." Among these Neanderthals crowding the comments was a random woman, one who did not follow me and wanted all of these men to know it. She wrote a comment criticizing my looks and insinuating I was ugly without the help of filters, because there's "no way she looks like that in real life."

The creator of this hateful video didn't acknowledge her comment, but he did respond to another one. A random man had responded to her commentary by saying, "You have a filter on your profile picture. So I would shut the fuck up if I were you." That comment was loved by the creator of the video. This woman that I had never met or interacted with engaged with vitriol targeted at me, and still got hit. Why? Because at the end of the day . . . she's a "bitch," just like me. No matter how many women you try to step on to be seen by the world's most mediocre men, you will never be taller than *any* man. You will always be one step below. And how can they respect you when they're always looking down at you?

In the previous chapter, I talked about how early gender socialization starts, how we have expectations for babies who aren't even born yet. And as children age into teenagerhood, which is when most people really begin to hone that sense of self-awareness, they become rudely, explicitly aware of the gendered power structures that make up our society.

The sad thing is that at its most effective, the patriarchy not only subjugates women and makes them believe they are less than, but also makes men into less empathetic, more close-minded versions of who they could be. In short, for the patriarchy to work, everyone gets hurt.

After all, if teenage girlhood is emotionally volatile, then teenage boyhood is a special kind of hell for *everyone* involved—combine puberty with a fragile male ego with the social dynamics of male camaraderie, and it's no surprise that mainstream American high school and college culture creates a hypermasculine environment—from fraternity houses to toxic hookup culture—that leads young boys to implicitly understand that they either uphold the patriarchy or become victims of it themselves (and we know why they tend to avoid the latter).

The first time I was ever asked for a nude was as a freshman in high school.

I was fourteen, and had just started school in a new county. I was very much the new kid compared to people who recognized one another from elementary or middle school. I had joined the volleyball team, and at my high school, the volleyball girls were part of the "popular" group, and I was very much looking forward to making a new circle of friends. I quickly became close with my fellow freshman and JV teammates, especially because we had to work the snack bar during every varsity game.

Pretty early on in the season, I was working one of these shifts when a boy walked up with his friends. Immediately, all the girls start giggling, and they start whispering about how cute and popular he had been in middle school, and that he was even cuter now. Even if he wasn't exactly my type, when I heard that, I was like, *Oh, word?* Because I guess if all the other girls liked him, then I should like him, too? Remember, I'm still a pick-me at this time, and thus concerned with male validation, especially if it comes from a boy that other girls are into.

To my delight, he starts talking to me and eventually asks for my number. I give it to him, of course. The minute he leaves, all the girls swarm me to congratulate me. *Oh my God, you're soooooo lucky!* I play it off to them, but inside I'm really feeling myself that this "popular" boy noticed me, because it must mean that I'm worth paying attention to . . . right?

He texts me later that night, and even though conversation at first is . . . uninspiring to say the least (imagine "hey." "hey." "sooo . . . what's up?" "not much, you?" back and forth for fifteen minutes), I'm still buzzing on the high of his attention. Which, of course, is when the conversation goes south.

First, he says, *you seem really cool, we should hang out sometime*, which obviously I giggle at. But then he texts, *I don't really remember what you look like, you should send me a picture so I never forget.*

Keep in mind this is all happening the same day, so in my head, I'm thinking, *It's been maybe five hours and you can't remember what I look like?* But okay. And then, bless teenage Drew's heart, because I send him a dorky selfie taken on my shitty flip phone, cheesing like a LinkedIn profile picture. I might even have thrown him a thumbs-up. Obviously, this is not what he's looking for, and we go back and forth a couple more times of him trying to ask in a roundabout way, with winky faces and *you know* . . . and me fully not knowing, because I was fourteen fucking years old and a child, before finally he loses patience and asks outright.

You should send me a nude. You should send me a picture of you naked.

That shocks me so much that I ask him why. Because I legitimately cannot understand why, one, he would want something like that; and, two, he thinks I'll actually send him one. And this idiot just responds, *so I can see.* Bro, what the fuck? How about you see DEEZ NUTS instead, pal?

When I refuse, he has the gall to say, *Why not? Don't be lame.* That's when I lose my temper, and I tell him, *Because I don't want to. And you DISGUST me.* And then he goes, *Whatever. You're not even that cute.*

The next day, I go to school and tell the story to my friends who had thought he was so cute and popular in middle school, which is also when I find out that *he's* been going around telling other kids in our grade that he doesn't like me because I'm a "fucking prude." That's what he called me. And when I heard that rumor, my response was "Tell him to come say that to my face."

Of course, he never did. In fact, he never talked to me again the next four years we were there. I like to think that was because, even then, he could tell I was not someone who spent much time talking if I felt disrespected.

When I think back to this incident, I can feel myself getting as angry as I did when it happened. We were fourteen fucking years old. It's infuriating that not only did he feel entitled enough to my body to ask me for nudes, but he then dared to call me a prude for not wanting to send them. As if he were *owed* that much from me. And the worst part is that I know this kind of shit happens all the time to girls even younger than I was, and with way worse repercussions. Even though it was traumatizing and infuriating that he called me a prude to our classmates, I also know that it's weird he didn't call me worse (and there would be boys who would call me, or my friends, worse for even lesser perceived transgressions).

When you see what boys are capable of, even at the young age of fourteen, is it any surprise that they eventually grow up to be the worst, most vile men?

This was one experience when my anger at being disrespected outweighed my fear of being disliked, but overall, my pick-me years are marred by countless little compromises that I made to my own self-respect or desires, all in the name of male validation or ego. Especially since, compared to when I was a kid, it seemed like the boys who I previously would've felt comfortable horsing around or being goofy with all started acting brand-new, like they couldn't be friends with us unless their crew of boys approved as well, and this new approval seemed rooted firmly in whether or not they thought we were "hot" or "cool," whatever the fuck that means at age fourteen.

At that age, adolescent Drew did not have a grasp on what sparked this transformation in boys she might have previously befriended with no qualms. All she knew was that there was an unspoken set of "rules" girls had to follow. A new set of rules that seemingly popped up overnight. What I know now and didn't realize then was that these were not new rules in any way—we were just finally becoming aware of the ancient code of patriarchy that we had been lucky enough not to be especially aggressively aware of until then.

In the face of this rude new awakening, I did come to the

realization that getting boys to like me was the strongest so-cial currency I could hold. And so, like every girl who came before me, and most likely every one of them who's come after me, too, I started to engage in the aforementioned pick-me behavior.

Especially when I transitioned from middle school to high school, it meant turning a critical eye on myself, and getting rid of or watering down any interests, outfits, opinions, or ideas that could get me into trouble with the guys, like hiding that I was a fangirl or dressing not for comfort but to look "cute." Trouble how? By annoying them, by being uncool, and by wanting anything other than what was intentionally catering to their collective preference.

It upsets me, remembering my behavior then, because I allowed shame and societal pressures to keep me from fully expressing myself. I wasted precious time worrying about what men who were far beneath me in every way believed about me. It breaks my heart that I felt like I needed to deny myself or make myself smaller, which is why I'm so unabashed about the things I love now. Because not only is that way of living extremely sad, but the longer that women engage in pick-me behavior and think so negatively of themselves and tra-ditionally female-aligned interests and behaviors, the more that judgment begins radiating outward and affecting the way they see and interact with other women. And then suddenly that misogyny is not only internalized, it's also externalized.

In the most extreme cases, you become like a manager I had when I had first entered the workforce in my early twen-ties, a woman who wanted so badly to be the only woman in a male-dominated industry—and a certain kind of woman, too—that she discouraged and undermined me at every opportunity she got. All my life, I've been really invested in personal style as a way to express myself, especially as a woman of color, and having been given an opportunity at this job, I was about to pull out all the stops in how I was dressed and how I was presenting myself at the office. For me, that meant makeup, nails, and lashes done. My manager, on the other hand, was always making microaggressive comments about my nails and lashes, clearly implying that my femininity and the ways I was choosing to express myself were unacceptable in the workplace. That they were a dog whistle for men to not take me seriously as a coworker, let alone an equal. And although I don't know for sure, I can't imagine I was the only young female employee she did that to—imagine how many women's professional dreams she probably destroyed in her quest to just sit in middle management forever, how many women she gaslit into believing they would never be good enough to sit at the table with all of their male counterparts, so they might as well give up (because there would only ever be enough room for one—her). Instead of mentoring, encouraging, or providing a safe space for me to accomplish all that she had or even more, especially in a male-dominated industry, she chose to go the scarcity route, believing that any accomplishment of mine meant one less opportunity for her.

But even in more subtle ways, it stands to reason that if you spend your entire life hyper-attuned to male interests, it will ultimately warp the way you see, present, and understand yourself. It may even lead you to question what you formerly thought were sincere interests, like my love of football. On the one hand, I knew intellectually that I loved it organically—my dad had played professionally, and football, as mentioned earlier, is a huge part of Samoan culture. On the other hand, it is also true that over the years, I have been rewarded for my love and knowledge of football by men who can't believe that a *woman* can know as much as I do. Did I even really . . . *like* . . . football? Or was this an elaborate, internalized misogynistic web that I had allowed to entangle my confidence, self-worth, and sense of accomplishment? I needed to be honest with myself, which I believe is truly a vital part of unpacking your internalized misogyny. After a lot of soul-searching and conversations with my therapist, I believe now that my love for football is legitimate. I know that might sound kind of silly—like really, I needed to spend that much time thinking about whether I love a sport I literally grew up around?—but I bring it up as an example of how deep the patriarchy can get under your skin, how subtly it can shape your life, and how it undermines even the most intrinsic, obvious parts of yourselves. Pick-me-ism is a disease. And if you don't nip it in the bud, it can be terminal, murdering any chance you have to live a life free from the shackles of male validation.

But although I always call out pick-me behavior, I try my best to understand the individual participating in it. Because I know just how difficult it is to go against something that is ingrained in literally every aspect of our society, and that everyone's journey to unlearning pick-me-ism starts at different points in their lives. And most importantly, it must start on their own terms. Judging any individual woman who isn't as far along on her path of recognizing this mindset doesn't help the process of understanding why she thinks she's better than other women because she allegedly likes football, beer, and blow jobs. As a result, parallel to my public vendetta against pick-me-ism and my desire to hold other women accountable for perpetuating and upholding oppressive systems, I have also learned the importance of practicing patience and compassion with women and femmes who display these behaviors . . . starting with my younger self.

When I look back at my pick-me years with all the knowledge and experience I have now of combating terrible men, I have to laugh. Adolescent Drew had literally no idea what she was up against, and still, she was doing the best she could with the tools in her teenage-girl arsenal. I don't blame her for falling into pick-me behavior—it's what made the most sense as a method of navigating the world of misogyny at such a young age. What I didn't realize while I was working so hard bending over backward to appeal to men is that the misogynistic, horrible men I was trying to impress were never going to respect me, no matter what I liked, how I dressed, or what I did. Because none of those things have anything to do with respect and being able to see yourself as an actual person with your own interests and opinions. I could scrub myself of all personality, fold myself into the tiniest box, and still there would be a horrible man who'd find me lacking in some way, because when men are misogynists, they hate *all* women, full stop. Not just "loud" and "angry" ones. Not just "slutty" ones. Not just "fat" ones. Not just "tall" ones. All of us. And if you identify as a woman in any capacity . . . that includes you. Every time. As much as I loathe the idea of having lived for male validation at one point in my life, I am grateful for one aspect of it: it opened my eyes. It gave me the gift of perspective and the confirmation that it truly never serves you to live for the enjoyment and pleasure of men.

At the same time, as I extend that compassion and understanding back to adolescent Drew and all young women and femmes experiencing similar struggles, I also have to remind myself to extend the same to boys of that age, who were similarly undergoing a period of immense pressure to conform. Contrary to what awful men believe about me or say online, I do actually understand that the patriarchy affects men, too. The irony in this situation being that they, as men, don't realize that an oppressive structure like the patriarchy sets up impossible standards to live up to on their end as well. What would help me would also help them. It is imperative that we all, regardless of how we identify, recognize the violent and persistent harm misogyny perpetuates in this world. It is so much deeper and more sinister and potentially catastrophic than it appears.

By that I mean, just think about how boys are socialized to be more aggressive and less emotionally expressive, or how there are strict parameters on how they should behave, dress, and act in order not to seem "girly." It creates an oppressive environment where anyone who does not conform to the cis heteropatriarchy is punished, and where one of the worst possible things is to exhibit behavior that is commonly ascribed to women. Imagine that filtered through playground misinformation or childhood cruelty, how it then trickles down to affect everyone in their path, and it becomes abundantly clear that under the patriarchy, it's not just women, femmes, trans girls, or queer kids who are hurt by these crushing expectations and rigid social norms, but also men.

The devil works hard, but the patriarchy works harder.

The thing I want to ask every grown woman who still participates in pick-me behavior is this: What has being a pick-me ever gotten you? What have you ever gained by actively pushing down women in order to be acknowledged by men? Male validation is the most useless and fleeting resource in the world. I can think of no instance where being a pick-me in high school or college kept me truly safe from the possibility of being an object of abuse, ridicule, ostracization, or objectification at the hands of men. It only staves it off for another day. Because ultimately, men will always close rank around their own, and in the most extreme pick-me scenarios, all you've done is alienate yourself from friends who could have supported, empowered, or comforted you. Being a pick-me means entering a cycle where aligning yourself with the patriarchy only means that when you become a victim of it—and you will—you'll be left without a support system. Without the comfort or safety of community. The system preys on the vulnerable, and if you think selling out your fellow girls for the attention of men is going to make you immune to it, you're a fool. And playing along with the patriarchy's game is no way to get out of it. As the writer and activist Audre Lorde wrote, "The master's tools will never dismantle the master's house."

So what will?

Let's review what we know: Pick-me behavior is easy to fall

into and near impossible to get out of if you aren't aware of your position. There isn't a simple five-step plan to eradicate it, as much as I wish there were. I can only promise that the journey to undoing the pick-me mindset, while difficult, can be the most freeing in the world if you persevere.

Why even bother undertaking it? Because I promise you: once you free yourself of the prison that a pick-me mindset traps you in, you will have unlocked the potential for greater happiness, confidence, and ability to connect on a deeper level than you have ever experienced before. It's what happens when you start living according to *your* desires, and not men's. It's the chance to silence men (even if it's just in your head), like men have done to us for thousands of years. It's the chance to feel free.

What helped me was identifying the one thing that has always been a true and intrinsic part of my character and up-bringing that is not aligned with being a pick-me—and be-lieve me, we all have one—and questioning if I was able to give that up just to be a more willing participant in the patriarchy.

Throughout my years of being a pick-me, that something had always been my commitment to being a girls' girl. There is something so magical and nourishing about female solidar-ity, love, and support, and having a strong group of female friends around me has always been nonnegotiable. Maybe it's because of Deison, because I'm the stubborn, know-it-all younger Virgo sister to my older sister's goofy, heart-on-her-sleeve Sagittarius and have gotten used to a lifetime of stand-ing up for her. Or maybe it's because of my mom, who drilled into my head that I could do anything I put my mind to, with or without a man, and built up my confidence by leading by example. Maybe it's because as much as I might have wanted male approval at one point in my life, I always knew that quality relationships, whether romantic or platonic, don't have a mismatched power dynamic that would put me in the position of having to constantly prove myself. Plus, female approval, or approval from someone who actually likes and respects you, feels a million times better than any fake, flimsy, and short-lived approval a man might offer you. Especially when men's approval is most often tied to an expectation of physical intimacy with them.

There are some pick-mes whose version of being "not like other girls" means denigrating them, acting one way privately and then speaking of them another way when men are present, or taking information told to them in confidence and sharing it with others in order to mock or gossip. Dishonesty is an especially heinous quality, in my opinion, but that kind of duplicitous behavior is really unacceptable to me. I sincerely mean it when I say that my mission is to uplift ALL femmes, which means holding space for the understanding that we are all, to some degree, victims of the patriarchy and, thus, each develop different coping mechanisms in response to it. However, grown women who buy into the patriarchy in a way that is actively misogynistic and harmful have my empathy, but not my respect. I see you, and I understand you're on your own journey, but at my grown age, or older, I think you have made a choice. You've chosen who to support and what to perpetuate, even if it violates women around you, and I will never understand that.

All my life, my closest, most loving, and most supportive

relationships have been with women and femmes, who are some of the smartest, kindest, most generous, and strongest people I have ever met. So how could I possibly believe that men were just better than them when I knew that was simply not true? That straightforward fact meant that it was becoming difficult to ignore the growing discrepancy between what I knew in my bones to be true of my friends and how the patriarchy expected me to treat my relationships with them, while also making peace with the way men treat us.

I once read about a study that stated that men die of suicide more often than women. However, the study actually only accounted for completed suicide attempts. In fact, men are more likely to go through with suicides, whereas women are far more likely to attempt but not actually complete the act (this only applies within the gender binary). The reason why women don't actually end up completing their suicides is because they attempt them in far less violent ways. According to the study, this is because women worry about family members or loved ones finding them and being traumatized by what they see. So they try less violent, and thus less final, ways—and therefore survive more often. Thinking about what an emotional load women carry every day purely because even at the end of their ropes they can't bear the thought of upsetting other people? It breaks my heart. It makes me angry. It strengthens my conviction. Women and femmes are necessary, valid in their emotions, and strong.

Which isn't to say that I didn't and don't have any quality male friends. But once my self-awareness around gender expectations started growing in middle and high school, I began to see how easily people went along with gendered behavior just because it was the safer thing to do. It would feel like a betrayal whenever a guy friend would treat me one way when we were alone and then turn on a dime the minute he was in the presence of other boys. Or the way he would insist he wanted nothing more from me other than friendship, but as soon as he admitted romantic feelings to me, the tides would turn if I didn't return the sentiment. Or the way mediocre men feel entitled to women, at any age and in any scenario, once they decide they're done cosplaying a platonic relationship. And even in spite of my brain being in the throes of my pick-me phase at the time, I knew *that* wasn't right. I knew I deserved better. And if that's how men saw friendship with women . . . who needs male friends at all? I think I knew on some elemental level that true friendship and mutual respect didn't look like folding myself into a smaller and smaller box, all for the approval of some guys who cared about appealing to the male gaze just as much as, if not more than, the ripest pick-me in the bunch.

I especially hated watching my girlfriends experience the same thing, and the cognitive dissonance of seeing girls who I knew were funny, smart, and amazing people feel diminished in the process of appealing to boys always made me protective of them and indignant on their behalf. And you know me—I'm a loud bitch who refuses to shut up, especially in the face of misogyny. So over time, whenever I saw my sister or one of our friends get hurt by some loser, I became the first and the loudest to tell them that he wasn't worth shit. This is how I developed a reputation for being the friend who you came to when you needed a pep talk or an insult for a creep that wouldn't leave you alone, a title that I wear with pride to this day.

As for how I began to realize just how at odds being a pick-me was with my desire for self-respect, it honestly came down to anger. In my own interactions with men, I began to realize that I needed to be a fucking bitch if I wanted men to take me seriously when I asked them to leave me alone, because being "nice" or trying to "let them down easy" meant that men saw that as a challenge, not the hard no that it was. It was impossible for me to sustain that level of disdain and not eventually begin to question just what I thought I was accomplishing by still trying to appeal to them. I realized that I was being a huge hypocrite in what I was saying versus what I was doing: If I thought most men were actually kind of horrible people, and I was going around proclaiming this to my friends, then why was I spending all this time pandering to them? How could I expect the women around me, whom I admire and love so dearly, to ditch these loser-ass men and truly see themselves as the bad bitches I saw, if I didn't hold myself to that same standard?

This was a huge revelation to me, and it really represents the first major step I took toward undoing my pick-me behavior. This was not a mental shift that happened instantaneously, but rather something that happened after observing way too many instances of men taking advantage of the kindness and vulnerability of women in all kinds of scenarios, not just interpersonal ones. There were countless examples: male teachers who didn't take female students seriously, male employers who treated female employees differently, male family members who had different expectations for the boy and girl cousins. I realized I needed to do more than just be a support for my girlfriends after the misogynistic damage was done. I needed men, the perpetrators of that hurt, to understand that their behavior was not okay, and that there would be repercussions for how they treated women. I needed them to know, even if they were unwilling to listen, not only that their behavior was unacceptable, but that I was never going to let it go unchecked ever again.

This desire to protect and uplift the women in my life is directly responsible for me finding my voice at a young age and for setting me on the difficult path of unlearning my own pick-me mentality. Now, as a reformed pick-me, I am immensely grateful that I had this foundational love for and drive to support women, which was formed by the amazing women who in turn loved and supported me. And once I started speaking out against terrible male behavior, I found that none of the things the patriarchy threatens will happen if you dare to defy it actually came to pass.

Doing the work of identifying and dismantling pick-me-ism has changed me for the better. My life is richer for it, and it has made me braver and more confident. It has helped grow my ability to give and receive love, because I no longer find myself in competition with others for a resource that I don't even want, like male approval. Support from women is a gift. It's a resource in which you can find not only community, but empowerment. It's a place you go to recharge and remind yourself that you are loved, important, and valid in this world. That's what it always has been for me, and that's what I always want it to be for all of you.

I can't tell you what your grounding belief will, or should, be, but trust me when I say that you have one, and that it has nothing to do with pleasing a man. And when you find it, it will transform you. My love for and solidarity with other women and femmes can never be taken away from me. They constantly give me the courage to brave this terrifying, daunting, beautiful, amazing world. When you let go of male validation, you not only take away all of their power, but also have the opportunity to redirect that power to yourself and others. Give yourself the permission to love yourself unconditionally, because there's nothing more radical in the eyes of the patriarchy than that . . . and we all know how much I love pissing off terrible men.

4

TRUST EXERCISE

I **am a firm believer** in having no regrets. Not just because I think regret can trap you and keep you spinning in unproductive circles, but also because I try not to do things or make decisions in the first place that I may come to regret. That means doing my best to always let love, solidarity, and support guide how I navigate this life.

I think the reason I'm so steadfast in this belief is because one of the biggest—and only—regrets is how I responded when one of the most important people in my life came to me looking for love and support, and I let them down in a big way.

I'm talking about Deison.

People who know me and my sister know that we're a package deal. I'm positive that my mom, my dad, the universe, and anyone else who looked at Deison the moment she was born must have thought to themselves, *That girl should be a big sister.* And lucky us, she became one two years later when I was born.

And she has been the best big sister to ever exist. I know a lot of people look at us and might be intrigued by our dynamic. I'm the loud, annoying, protective one, and my sister is the shy, sensitive, sweet one. And they'd be right to a certain extent, but the truth is that Deison has taught me so much about being true to yourself. She inspires me to want to be a better person, because she's one of the best people I've ever met.

Like I mentioned, Deison was only a year ahead of me in school even though she was two years older. So we've been attached at the hip from the moment I was born, and all throughout elementary, middle, and high school. We've always had similar interests in everything from fandom to activities, and while we obviously each had our own friends, we still shared a close circle until college, when she went to the University of Oregon, and I went to the University of Hawai'i at Manoa.

When she left for college in the fall of 2012, that first semester was the longest and farthest we'd been apart in our entire lives. Even if we talked basically every day (and this was pre-FaceTime, so we were on Skype and ooVoo all the time—remember them?) and she came home for every holiday, it was different from how we used to spend all our time together.

Though I may not seem like it, I've always been a typical little sister in more ways than not. When we were growing up, whatever Deison did, I wanted to do, too. Everything she liked, I liked, too. And because we were so close in age, we went through many milestones back to back, like first crushes, first periods, first weird dates to school dances, you name it. Deison and I had no secrets—or so I thought.

In the months leading up to spring 2013, I was impatient and excited, not only for my own high school graduation but for Deison's return to being a constant presence in my life.

When she came home in May, it felt like a return to our old dynamic, and I was so relieved. To me, it meant that our relationship was strong and that it would withstand any change. I didn't have to worry about leaving for Hawai'i in the fall, because I knew Deison and I would always fall right back into the swing of being sisters the moment we reunited. I was so happy. After all, it was summer, and my favorite person was home.

One day, Deison asked me to go to the beach. The beach is a few hours from where we lived, and even though I love the beach, I know she doesn't, so it definitely made me think something might be up. She drove the three of us (including my nine-year-old brother) down there. While Donovan played in the sand and we were lying out on beach towels, she finally said she had something to tell me. I had a gut feeling that what she wanted to talk about had to do with dating, because that had been a major theme of our conversations that year, but what she shared with me caught me totally off guard.

She told me that she had been dating a girl she met playing rugby. They had been dating for eight months. She was gay.

Even if I'd had an inkling that she wanted to tell me something about her dating life, this was absolutely not what I'd expected. After all, this was my sister, who I had known my entire life. She was someone who I thought I knew better than anyone, and at the young age of seventeen, sometimes I thought I knew her even better than I knew myself. As her self-appointed protector and her biggest supporter, I saw her best qualities even when she didn't want to believe them about herself, and if you had asked me then or now, I would say with full confidence that the relationship we have is one of complete trust and understanding.

And yet, when she chose to entrust me with this revelation about herself, I let her down in a big way.

My response, initially, was shock. Even as she was fighting back tears from how tense the situation was, I just got up and left her on the towels so I could go for a long walk on the beach. And I'm ashamed to say that the entire time I was walking, what I was thinking about was . . . myself. How hurt I was, and how betrayed I felt. Instead of listening to what she was trying to tell me about who she was, all I could think about was what a shock this was to the version of Deison I believed she was. Deison had always crushed on boys when we were growing up, even if she had notoriously bad taste in them (though maybe in retrospect that was a sign all along . . .), so to learn that she was gay *and* that I'd had no inkling of it emphasized all the change she'd gone through in college without me. This was my sister, who I had never hid a secret from. And for her to have hidden a whole-ass relationship from me? In retrospect, I can see that she had probably kept her feelings to herself because it was something she wanted to work through on her own before sharing with other people. And as close as we were—as close as anyone is to anyone else—I wasn't entitled to know her feelings or firsthand experiences in life. I was just privileged to be able to share them with her. I wish I had realized this at the time.

After the shock, I was hurt, because I'd been asking my sister all year while she was away at college if she'd had any crushes, if she was dating anyone, what dating in college was like, etc., and she'd never have anything to report. So for her to not only come out to me, but also reveal that she was in a relationship and had been for eight months *and* that she'd already told our mom: I felt betrayed. That sentence, even now, a decade later, makes me cringe to write. To think that the entire time my sister was being incredibly brave in sharing this with me, I was centering my own feelings . . . it's embarrassing. All I was doing was thinking about myself, while she waited for me to show up. I let her down, and to this day I hate myself for it. Looking back, not to excuse my behavior at all, but I think the reason I reacted this way was because it made me feel like not only had she lied to me about her feelings and her life, she was having all these experiences without me.

But at the time, it was impossible for me to express all these warring emotions. And even though I would've considered myself a very open-minded and accepting person, my response to Deison's coming-out highlights just how ignorant I actually was. Instead of talking to her, I completely shut down.

When I finally came back from my walk, all I had to say to her was that I wanted to go home. She tried to apologize, and even said, "I wasn't trying to ruin the day." Instead of comforting her, even though she'd clearly been crying, all I said was "I just want to go home. I don't want to be here anymore."

We drove home in dead silence, Donovan asleep in the

back seat and neither Deison nor I speaking. I remember Deison was crying, and swirled in with my own selfish feelings of hurt and confusion was anger. A small part of it was because I felt lied to, and because I didn't understand why she chose this time to tell me, but mostly it was because I realized that she was in pain, that I was the one causing her pain, and yet I couldn't get out of my own way and be there for her. Obviously, I know now that there is no perfect time to come out to someone. Moreover, it shouldn't be on the person who is coming out to create a safe and secure environment. So the fact that I sat there stewing in my own emotions rather than affirming something that Deison clearly needed a lot of courage and faith to share with me is a choice I will rue having made until the day I die.

If I could go back in time and fix anything, it would be that day and that car ride. And I would fill that silence with love and reassurance and support. I would tell her how valid and important she is, and reassure her that who she loves will never impact how much I love her. My heart aches, thinking of how absent I was in a moment when she needed me most.

I recognize that this was an incredibly selfish and hurtful response to my sister's act of true courage and trust. It's still difficult to fully parse all the competing emotions I was feeling at that time—not because I want to make my sister's coming-out about me in any way, but because I want to pinpoint just how I let her down so I never do it again. I do know there's a lot of shame attached to that memory. Because Deison is not just my sister, she's my best friend and my whole world. All my life, all I've wanted is for her to be happy and fulfilled, and in the exact moment when it would've mattered most to express that, I wasn't able to.

When we got home, Deison parked the car and let Donovan go ahead of us into our house before breaking the silence. She asked if I had any questions, and even though usually I'm such a loudmouth and have a million questions about everything, this time I just said, "No." She asked if I was still in shock, if I wanted to talk, or if I needed space from her. And I just told her, "I don't know. I just don't want to talk."

After that car ride, we didn't talk for a few days, which is possibly the only time in our lives that has ever happened—and if I can do anything about it, it will stay the only time in our lives that will ever happen. My parents were certainly aware of the tension, but ultimately, this was between Deison and me. Reconciliation couldn't be forced, and it would have to come from me.

The next time we had a conversation was on our way to a family function. Our parents maneuvered it so that they took Donovan, and Deison and I were left to drive there together. And again, she just asked me if I had anything I wanted to ask her, and I just said no. Then she asked if I wanted her to go back to Oregon early. This broke me. It truly made me feel like the worst person in the world—because I was being exactly that. Even while she was hurting, she wanted to make space for me and prioritize my comfort at the expense of her own. She wanted to give me the chance to feel my emotions and ask questions with no judgment. And her empathy for my internalized biases that I had yet to unpack makes me so emotional to think back on. Why was she having to do this labor for both of us? What was preventing me from simply being supportive in a moment when she needed it most?

But even after this conversation, I still wasn't able to be the person Deison needed me to be. We were talking again, but the conversations were few and far between, and so forced and superficial that it was just awful. We were existing around each other, but barely. She was keeping to herself to give me space, so that I could come to her when I was ready. That almost supernatural sister connection that had existed so strongly between us all our lives had been disrupted, and the worst part was that I had been the person to do so.

I don't know if there was an actual moment that snapped me back into reality or if I just missed her so much that I couldn't take the tension anymore, but there was a point in the middle of the summer when I realized how insane it was that I hadn't really seen or talked to her even though we were literally living in the same house. I missed her. I loved her. What was I doing?

When I realized that, it forced me to take a look at myself and the way I'd been behaving. I had to really ask myself, what was I so upset about? About her being gay? About her keeping her relationship from me? So what? What did any of that matter if I really loved her the way I thought I did? Were her choices hurting me or affecting me, or did they even have anything to do with me, in any way?

And the answer finally came: of course not. Deison had exercised immense courage and trust by coming out to me, and especially given our dynamic growing up, where she was often more cautious and I was fearless, this felt like a role reversal: now she was the brave one, and I was the one who needed to face the situation head-on. Of course, what it also taught me is that being strong and brave doesn't just mean having the quickest clapback or the sharpest words, which is how I'd always operated, but being steadfast and true to yourself, which is what Deison has always done.

I finally realized that, more than anything, Deison needed to know she had my unconditional love and support, and that I'd be in her corner moving forward, the same way that I always had been.

But even after I'd come to that realization, it was hard for me to express it all to Deison. At first, I just tried to treat her like normal without apologizing or even acknowledging that the past few weeks had happened. She understandably was resistant because it must've been confusing for her to see me go from one extreme to another. After a few days of this, I knew that I needed to display even 1 percent of the courage she had, and finally apologize to her.

The next time I knew we were both alone in the house, I approached her and asked to talk. I shared my feelings of hurt, fear, and anger, and finally asked her the question I should've asked all along. "Are you happy?" When she said, "Yeah, I'm in love," it honestly just made me feel even worse. Because what the fuck had I been doing all this time? My sister was trying to share her happiness and her new love with me, and I had responded by icing her out for weeks.

She told me that in those weeks we weren't speaking, she was so afraid that my reaction meant that I didn't love her anymore, or that I thought she was disgusting. Even writing that out makes me tear up, because I can't believe that not only was I responsible for making someone feel that way, but

I was responsible for making *Deison*, the most important person in my life, feel that way.

The beautiful thing about Deison is that she is an incredibly loving and patient person. Where I am quick to anger and prone to suspicion, Deison has a seemingly bottomless ability to hold space for others. Even in this situation, where I was responsible for causing her such hurt, she let me come to her on my own time, and never stopped loving me all the while. Even as we were having the conversation where I was *finally* getting around to acknowledging the hurt I'd caused her, she still told me, "I don't ever have to talk about it around you if that makes you uncomfortable." Which shows just how big her heart is, that even in that moment she was still thinking about my comfort.

She asked me if I still loved her, and even though I hate that I made her doubt that, I'm glad I got a chance to tell her, full on, that I love her. Of course I do.

Not too long after, I realized I hadn't actually apologized for how I had initially responded. So I sat down with her and was able to finally apologize and convey my sincere regrets for how I had handled it. I needed her to know that my love for her was eternal and unconditional, and that the only thing that mattered to me—the only thing that has *ever* mattered to me—was that she was happy, safe, and loved.

It's not that it was all kumbaya after that, since you can't expect a relationship to bounce back immediately after such an egregious hurt, but my apologizing and acknowledging the harm was at least the first step in the process of patching that small, but avoidable and insidious, hole I had created in our relationship. To this day, I'm grateful that Deison chose to forgive me. It's not something I will ever take for granted.

That lapse in my own judgment, however momentary, is what made me acutely aware of how important it is to be very firm about what you believe and what you stand for. And how being a true intersectional ally means being proactive and willing to learn/unlearn, no matter how long it takes. Otherwise you might end up hurting the very people you're trying to protect. Up until that point, I absolutely would've said I was so liberal and so open, and yet it's clear that my conviction had never been tested. In a situation where I was faced with a real opportunity to step up and actually be there for someone, I responded with fear and doubt purely caused by internalized homophobia.

Even after I had apologized to Deison, I realized that showing her true acceptance meant so much more than just saying so. I still remember that even after my apology, when we were starting to get back into our old rapport, Deison was very reserved when it came to how much she talked about her girlfriend. I realized that she was worried I was uncomfortable, and that it was on me to proactively ask questions about her girlfriend the same way I had when she had crushes on boys in the past or that I would ask of any friend's boyfriend. I realized that even asking mundane questions like *What does she study? What does she want to do? What is her family like?* meant a lot to Deison. It was time for me to unpack my internalized biases, many of which I hadn't even realized existed.

It also wasn't until later that I acknowledged there was also a very real fear for Deison's safety that informed the way I had responded to her coming-out. The world is an evil, bigoted place, and though I knew our immediate family, friends, and peers would be accepting, the threat of homophobic violence was then and still remains very real. My fear for her well-being and happiness, coupled with her very existence simply being threatened by her loving who she wants, filled me with a dread I couldn't possibly articulate at that time. I was afraid, and emotionally unequipped to share that fear in a way that still prioritized Deison in that moment.

But I regret that I let anxiety about how others would respond shape how I reacted. I was scared that moving through the world as an out queer woman would alienate my sister. Out of a twisted sense of protection, I remember that in that very first conversation on the beach, the only things I could ask her were "What do you mean?" and "Are you sure?" Which are such ignorant, invalidating questions to ask of someone who's just come out. Even if they might have come from a well-intentioned place of not wanting my sister to have to navigate the pain and difficulty that were likely to lie ahead, at the time, I was questioning her identity and her experience right at the moment in which she finally felt brave enough to open up to me.

That moment really taught me the difference between intention and impact. That is to say, while your intentions are certainly important, what's more important is how your actions impact the other person. Every interaction has two people, so it matters how *both* people feel, not just one. But this seemingly simple concept is one of the hardest for people to grasp, and I've seen everyone from friends and loved ones to terrible men jump on the defensive when confronted with their own words. "But I didn't mean to hurt you!" That's great, but you did, so what will you do about it now?

Years after that conversation, long after Deison had become comfortable living in her own identity around my family, some of my initial fears when Deison came out to me became very real. In 2016, when it became clear that Trump might have a chance of winning the upcoming presidential election, there was a violent shift in the platforming of bigoted ideology on social media. I was surprised and disgusted by the opinions I saw being shared by people on my feeds, people I had thought I knew.

My entire family and I had to make some serious changes to who we associated with. With Deison being a proud gay person and the rest of my family and me being devoted allies, we had to draw our line in the sand with these bigots. My sister led the charge. Deison drew her line and cut them off, no matter if they were blood family, friends, or others. And I was right there with her. Because Deison is my person. No matter who I'm up against, even if they're prejudiced family members, I don't care. I choose her, every single time.

That moment of hesitation when Deison came out to me is why I will be loudmouthed and opinionated until the day I die, and why I will always call out misogynistic, homophobic, or any other bigoted bullshit whenever I see it, whether that's in person or online. I never risk letting someone else make others, let alone people I personally know and love, feel the way I might've made Deison feel. Even if it means losing fans, friends, professional opportunities, or even family because I am too straightforward about my beliefs, then so be it and good riddance.

In the years to come, I would feel empowered by how my sister's sexuality changed the way she thought about herself and her relationship to people of all gender identities, and enabled her to create a new lens through which to view the world. It also made me realize that so many structures that we accept as "standard" or as the "status quo" are actually secret tools of the patriarchy, like compulsory heterosexuality, which assumes that all people are automatically straight until proven otherwise. The heterosexual patriarchy means that we set up a dynamic where *of course* boys are the ones who are crushed on, while girls do the crushing. And *of course* we assume all young women have crushes on men, because under the patriarchy, a relationship that doesn't center or involve men at all is unimaginable and invalid.

Learning more about queerness and the LGBTQIA+ community also forced me to face my own toxic beliefs, and made me realize that as much as I was a budding man-hater, there was still so much I did not know. Like the distinctions between the female and male gazes.

If these are unfamiliar concepts to you, don't worry, because they were unfamiliar to me, too. And yet learning about them really helped me understand how subtly our world and our viewpoints become gendered. The terms come from film theory: the male gaze means that there is not only an assumption that the person behind the camera is male, but there is also an assumption that the audience is male, and so everything is framed in a way that appeals to men. Unfortunately, that means viewing women as sex objects, people to be conquered, or tropes, which is how you might get one-dimensional or overtly sexual portrayals of women in media or culture.

Now consider how everything we see around us and consume is filtered through this gaze, and it's no wonder that women begin to internalize the male gaze, too. It's something that I've been guilty of for sure, especially when I was younger. When I was still unpacking my internalized misogyny, I realized that some of the outfits I used to wear were almost exclusively meant to appeal to the male gaze (ew). Even though I might have enjoyed wearing those outfits of my own volition sometimes, I simultaneously understood that one of the main reasons I chose to wear them was an attempt to come across as "hotter" to men. And because, unfortunately, I am still attracted to men, the logic follows that I *should* wear what would appeal to them. In relationships between men and women, the patriarchy dictates that desire should always flow in a certain direction, and it should always involve the woman trying to get the man's attention. Our culture itself is all tied up in the pick-me dynamic, because ultimately it's all geared toward men and what they want.

It can even affect how straight women view other women—think about the snap judgments that someone may make based on how a woman presents herself, and how often these judgments are made based on a perception of how that woman may look to a man. For example, when a woman says that another woman looks slutty or, on the flip side, like "she's really let herself go," I always have to wonder what perspective that judgment is being made through. Whatever women and femmes do, it's simply never enough in the eyes of the patriarchy.

The female gaze, on the other hand, means women are given autonomy in crafting their own images for a female audience. That's why learning about the female gaze was revelatory to me. Because it turns out that if you start to see the world through a female gaze, women are valued for much more than their looks or their sex appeal, but for their thoughts and emotions. Their drive, ambitions, and passions. They're *seen* and represented for who they truly are, which is a much more complex portrait than how they look.

The female gaze allows for the apparently groundbreaking concept that women don't exist just to further a man's narrative or character development and that women are not only mommies or girlfriends or mommy-girlfriends, but individuals with distinct personalities and specific desires. It's what formed the foundation of my body neutrality approach, where I aim to think of my body as a utilitarian vessel where the most interesting parts of myself, my thoughts and beliefs, are housed, and nothing more.

Bearing witness to Deison's unlearning of the male gaze as it affected not only herself but the women she was attracted to challenged beliefs that I had thought were foregone conclusions. As I watched Deison become more confident in herself once she was freed from some of the heteropatriarchal expectations that had been placed on her to live a certain way, and explore relationships that were a thousand times more nuanced than those with any of the boys she had crushed on in high school, I realized that there was an incredible power in decentering men, especially the invisible male spectator.

As my community grew, it came to include many individuals from the LGBTQIA+ community, and learning from them how they talked about and approached desire was instrumental in helping me unpack my own understanding of it. Being open-minded about all the different forms love can take has made my life richer and my existing relationships more meaningful. It's why I have zero tolerance for homophobia and transphobia on top of misogyny, and why I will fight for the LGBTQIA+ community as hard as I fight for women and femmes (which are obviously not mutually exclusive communities).

In fact, being able to see how people create loving environments and relationships, despite being targeted and vilified for it, helped me understand how much happier one can be when not conforming to patriarchal expectations. And because members of the LGBTQIA+ community often have to form tight-knit friendships and found-family structures with one another, it's inspired me to invest deeply in my nonromantic relationships. That's what's provided the foundation of feeling like I'd be okay even if I ended up alone, without a romantic relationship, because the friends, family, and community I surround myself with are more than enough. I don't need to let a horrible man into the equation just to feel loved. I am already plenty loved without that.

My understanding of the scope of what's possible for women in this world and what's truly worth valuing in ourselves completely evolved during this time. It's why I am now so steadfast and so loud and vocal in my support for women and femmes: because I know the power of speaking up. I never want *anyone* to have to guess at what I feel, which is why being the loudest person in a room is a compliment to me. It's why I don't give a shit if you think my content is alienating, and why I say good riddance to all the people who say they used to be a fan of me but then I got to be "too much" or went "too far" in my support for *all* women and femmes, no matter their race, sexuality, or gender identity. If you're a homophobe, transphobe, or TERF and you don't like me, guess what? The feeling is mutual.

I'm hoping that not everyone will need the experience of disappointing someone they deeply care about, like I did, to understand what it means to have your important relationships evolve and for you to evolve alongside them. Because it's one of the easiest things in the world to allow rifts to appear between you and the people you care about out of fear of changing or admitting you're wrong.

Although I wish I could go back in time and make the choices that wouldn't hurt one of the people I care about most, I did learn the value of not centering myself and my feelings. I learned how to step outside of my own narrow viewpoint in order to actually show up for other people.

Good thing, too, because it turns out that when you center only yourself, you risk losing everyone else.

5

THE FALLACY OF "LEFTOVER WOMEN," AND OTHER MISOGYNISTIC MYTHS

One of the reasons why the patriarchy feels insidious and impossible to combat is because it tricks people into thinking that it's merely part of our social fabric rather than something that we are indoctrinated into believing. Remember Donald Trump in the lead-up to the 2016 election and his behavior onstage during his debates with Hillary Clinton? Snide under-the-breath comments whenever she spoke, following her around and getting all up in her personal space, denying facts and making up stories. That was the year the term "gaslighting" entered the national lexicon—it would take until 2022 for it to be named Merriam-Webster's Word of the Year, but that's only because "surreal" won out in 2016 instead—and it was wild to see the worst parts of the patriarchy physically embodied in one man who, you know, actually went on to become the president. It's still fucking surreal thinking about how we let that happen.

Trump's behavior would've been familiar to anyone who'd been through an abusive relationship. He deployed some of the most effective scare tactics in a misogynist's arsenal, from undercutting a woman's authority to straight-up lying. He's outwardly and unapologetically misogynistic, and a whole bunch of terrible men love him for it. Even if they don't necessarily seem violent or harmful (which they are; emotional and verbal abuse are still very much valid forms of abuse), it's critical to examine the shared thought pattern that bonds these men and their beliefs.

It turns my stomach to think about what terrible, bigoted men find camaraderie in, but I realize their default frame of mind is to violate and invalidate women, and I've noticed they all share the same trite, black-and-white thinking pattern when it comes to female behavior, which they believe should first and foremost cater to and be palatable to men. They think that's how *ALL men feel about women* and that it's on women to *pull it together or die alone.* More broadly, their refusal to acknowledge femmes outside of archaic gender roles is expected to work as a sort of scare tactic that'll tighten their hold on women, and their boldface messaging points to the underlying current of aggression that many of us experience in our daily lives.

This chapter aims to identify the kinds of lies and misogynistic myths that the patriarchy attempts to trap us with, so you, reader, can be on the lookout for everything from insidious microaggressions to straight-up violence. I'll challenge you to examine the behaviors you might just be accepting as "normal" but are actually inherently problematic. Together, we'll unpack the more nuanced lies the patriarchy uses in its attempt to brainwash us into subordination, and the power we can gain from not only identifying it early on but also laughing in its face.

Myth 1: The "Leftover Women" Dilemma

A popular train of thought among misogynists and their cronies goes as follows: *Young women get to date who they want while men date who they can. But when they get older, men marry who they want and women marry who they can.*

There's a fallacy perpetuated in society that women who are unwilling to compromise their standards will have to endure a huge scramble at the "end" of their lives to try to find a husband. That they'll be the "leftover" ones. And we're talking about women in their thirties, forties, and fifties who just happen to be unmarried. These are women in their prime who have done nothing but commit the apparent crime of letting experience and age give them the wisdom and strength to not settle for less. God forbid, am I right?

This is nothing more than an attempt at gaslighting us into settling for someone less than impressive. It's a narrative terrible men use to try and manipulate women and weaponize any desire we may have to one day marry and start families against us. They want us to believe that we simply have no time to hold out for better and that if we don't give in now, we'll probably be alone for the rest of our lives. It's a trick to convince us we'll never find anyone better, one that reduces women to biological clocks. Because what even is the point of being a woman if the goal isn't to settle with a man who may or may not deserve you, and have children that you may or may not want? If women really knew what they were capable of, and who they were capable of getting romantic interest from, where would that leave terrible men? The correct answer is *in the lurch*.

If you're currently single, or seeing someone but unbothered about planning a future together, instead of worrying about one day being a "leftover" woman, celebrate being left alone. Can you actually imagine anything good coming from a life being trapped with someone who you know isn't deserving of that level of commitment? Do you want to waste what little time we have on this earth giving love to someone who doesn't see you as a human, much less an equal? You've already made it this far with the person whose relationship should be the most important in your life: yourself. You will always be better off alone than guilted into a partnership with someone who you're not totally set on out of fear that there simply isn't enough time left for you in life to go after whatever, and whomever, you truly want.

Instead of indulging in limiting beliefs that put you at a disadvantage, defy the judgment that's placed on women and challenge the idea set forth that we will run out of options later in life. If you don't find it by the time you reach thirty or the time you reach forty, who is to say it might not still be out there for you to find by fifty, sixty, or seventy? I may not know what your soulmate looks like, I may not know when you will meet them or where, but one thing I do know? You'll never find them if you give in to these patriarchal societal pressures and settle for what you *don't* want.

Myth 2: Men Are "Naturally" Business-Minded and Domestic Labor Is "Women's Work"

Let's get one thing straight: women and femmes have boundless consumer power. When it comes to what's trending, flying off the shelves? It's up to the girls. Marketers adore brands and products with all-female demographics because women move units. We not only buy shit, but we follow you, we decide if you go viral, we talk about you, we promote you (whether it's a product or a platform), and we make sure you know how loved you are. We are an integral cog in what's popular. Women will follow what they love to the ends of the earth. If you can get the girls on your side, you can do anything.

And men hate that.

Seeing a woman like me being herself online and earning financial, social, and professional rewards for doing something that not only directly opposes their misogyny, but continues to build her career, makes them absolutely livid. I make a living off of hurting their fucking feelings. It's the greatest Uno Reverse they never saw coming.

Jokes aside, I do believe the biggest issue with only men being hyped up from a young age to believe that they will become financially successful and powerful in business, while young girls and women are encouraged to succeed in looks, love, and relationships, is that it ultimately perpetuates serious issues of inequality in domestic partnership.

In the 2010s, while my peers and I were in high school, college, and just entering the professional world, there was a ton of messaging that urged young women to strive for careers and to actively seek out opportunities to *crush it* in the workplace. We were being urged to *lean in* and *girlboss* our way to the top so we could one day dismantle the C-Suite boys' club. Again, it's quite possible this influx of media branded at female professional empowerment occurred *because* women were such eager consumers of it and desperate to get their hands on some answers and a road map to finding success in a man's world.

Or maybe all the men at the head of the table realized that women were going to pursue advancement in the workplace either way, so they might as well make money off of their incessant pursuit of some sense of equality. In any case, these messages often failed to offer inclusionary solutions and were, in many instances, still pitting women against one another in pick-me fashion. As much as this brand of girlboss feminism somewhat acknowledged the prevalent patriarchal structures that pervade business culture, its solutions remained alarmingly individualistic: work your ass off and be better than everyone else. It didn't offer a new way forward so much as empty motivational speech for enduring the system already in place.

But I digress. For all the girlboss era's shortcomings, we cannot forget to hold men accountable, too. While all of this was going on, no one was doing any work on the minds of the young men in my generation to rebrand the value of domestic labor, child-rearing, and caregiving, all traditionally women's roles. These duties have always been, and still remain, thankless work that carries no social reward or monetary incentive, so why would men envision it for themselves? Raising a child and keeping a household are arguably some of the most difficult and most important things you could ever do, but men continue to evade such work because it's never been presented at any point in Western culture as being "for" them. It's only ever been labeled "women's work." They can shirk these important responsibilities because it's not an issue if they don't show up around the house. It'll probably still get done without their help, and if it doesn't, no one's going to blame them, only their female counterparts, for failing to keep the household together.

It's not lost on me that the near superpower business acumen of many successful female founders, leaders, and entrepreneurs may in fact be a by-product of being pushed beyond limits they never thought imaginable. Take my mom, for example. When she had my sister and me, she was barely in her twenties and absolutely terrified, but kept her faith that she would figure it out. She was an amazing, hardworking mom and woman, even at twenty-two. She never had to go it alone, but my dad's career with the NFL did leave her in a position at certain points where she had to work, go to school, take care of us, and be a supportive spouse all at once. My dad always wrote letters, sent money and gifts to remind us he was thinking of us, called us as much as the technology in the early 2000s would allow, and came home when he could, but for a few years the vast majority of parenting responsibility unquestionably fell on my mom. She did everything in her power to keep our family strong even when we were struggling, both financially and logistically, to keep it all together and running smoothly.

As soon as my dad's run with the pros came to an end, he moved back home and immediately jumped into working various odd jobs so he could continue to provide for our family. He's been an IT guy for a manufacturing company, a personal trainer, a mover, a bouncer, and a courthouse sheriff, just to list a few. But at that point, my mom was on track to make huge gains in her career, having worked her way up the corporate ladder into a high-paying job in public relations.

It was an easy call: my dad would handle things at home with the kids, including all the cooking, cleaning, and housework, while my mom put in long hours in her new executive position at the firm. The domestic role reversal that they needed to execute to keep our family going could not have been more seamless. My dad completely empowered and supported my mom without a trace of resentment. He still does, and she's remained the main breadwinner in our family ever since.

The truth is, we're very lucky, and while I would love for this behavior to be normal, I'm well aware that it's not. I talk a lot about Samoan culture being one that's more matriarchal at its core, but the patriarchy is inescapable. There's still a strong belief that men should earn a paycheck while women stay at home, or, far more frustratingly, even when *both* earn a paycheck, all of the domestic and emotional labor *still* falls on the women. Samoan men can be just as bad when it comes to making assumptions about gender roles, because one thing colonization has in spades is its ability to implant patriarchy in every culture it touches. And I have never lost sight of how strong and resilient my parents had to be to never listen to anyone but themselves when it came to how they wanted to run their household and uphold each other as equal partners.

If there's any silver lining, it's this: the very foundation of entrepreneurship rests on the belief that you can take it all upon yourself and that no job is beneath you. Going out on your own and starting an empire, or working your way up a steep, prejudiced corporate ladder, is not for the faint of heart. It requires complete immersion and dedication, and no one has ever gotten there without working their ass off, regardless of what they identify as. Women and femmes are unafraid of thankless work and are no strangers to being underestimated, unaccommodated, and pushed beyond our capabilities, all while being forced to walk the tightrope of being ambitious and hardworking while also not being perceived as a "bitch." Our labor is often invisible, but we're *always* working . . . and most of the time with a smile on our face (real or not, misogynists can never tell). And this is because, I've said it before and I'll say it again, *women run shit.*

Myth 3: Girls Are Drama

We've all been there. We've all known the girl—and quite a few of us have been that girl at some point, too (myself included, I'll admit)—who claims, "All my friends are guys because girls are drama." It's a common pick-me trope, sure, but it's also a lie. Any kernel of truth to this belief only stems from society's desire to pit women against one another. They want us to believe that we are in direct competition with one another for every win in life, that there can only ever be one of us who comes out on top, and the prize at the end of this self-hatred rainbow? *Male validation* . . . yuck.

This trope is exactly why I refuse to vilify other women on my platform, especially in the same way I eviscerate men. I know, deep down, that they've lost their way. They believe that by denying themselves the joy of reveling in sisterhood and removing themselves from any kind of female solidarity or community, they might get into the boys' club. They might actually evade the perverse and incessant abuse of men if they choose to betray their fellow women for their approval. But this belief is like a mirage in the desert: the closer you think you're coming to it, the farther away it moves. It's not real or based in reality, it's a tactic to keep you chasing something misogynistic men are never willing to give you . . . respect as an equal.

Believe me when I say that there is nothing about that existence I covet, and I feel deeply sad for the women who end up there because there's nothing in this world I've been able to accomplish without having other women by my side. From my mom, who is right there with me (I'm talking *in the boardroom*, jotting down notes) every single time I negotiate a new business deal, to my sister, who was my emotional rock throughout the transition of putting my life online and who has become a creative partner in my brand, to my friends from sports teams, dorm rooms, and waitress jobs throughout high school and college, some of whom I've known for over a decade, who still come out to see me and celebrate together whenever I do live shows in their town, I never would have found who I truly am if it weren't for those tight-knit relationships with other women. Women have profoundly shifted and fast-tracked my road to self-confidence and discovery.

And while I know there's nothing I can personally do to change the minds of women who don't like me because they've chosen to side with and defend misogynistic men, I do hope they will eventually see the fault in their logic and realize that joining men in belittling other women will never change the fact that they are still women, and when men rally around their own, that never includes us. The decision to sell out for the approval of mediocre men will often come at the expense of all women, whether they realize it or not. In addition to this kind of behavior being packaged in a pretty self-sabotaging bow, cultivating friendships with men is also just as, if not *way* more, emotionally taxing than showing up for the girls. You've all seen how unhinged sensitive men get when I call them ugly or tell them they look like they work the closing shift at AutoZone after they bully marginalized people on the internet. *They* are drama!

They don't want you on their team. You think that because they give you short-term validation they're going to respect you any more than they respect a woman like myself? They won't. At the end of the day, you still are "othered" by them; you still don't belong. You are still less than them in their eyes. If they hate women, that *includes you*. You don't make the cut either (even as a pick-me). Life without allies, and just prioritizing men in general, is flat, colorless, and pointless. Trying to cater to men all the time will not only hold you back, but always harm you in some way or other, in the end.

While feeling competitive is somewhat natural—it's true that our evolutionary instincts can cause us to feel intimidated by other women who we share goals and similar interests with—this emotion is heavily exploited by the patriarchy and is made so much worse by the limiting belief, and in some cases the very harsh reality, of scarce opportunities for women. We're all exhausted living this way, but giving in to societal structures that pit us against one another only sustains the self-fulfilling prophecy that there can only be one woman in the room for every ten to twenty men. But with all the systemic issues working against women and people of color, we cannot afford to sacrifice our relationships with one another.

Cutting other women out of our lives with the expectation that it will propel us to opportunities for advancement typically reserved for men is not the solution. It's a smoke screen that'll distract you from setting true goals for yourself about where you want to be. If your professional strategy is seeking the validation of men, or putting down women who are lateral to you in order to appear more capable to these men, in hopes that they will bestow upon you their approval and permission to move up in the world, you're resigned to giving yourself no real agency whatsoever.

We are capable of so much, and we have to look out for and support one another to offer protection against casual misogyny and disrespect, in the world in general, but especially in environments like work or school (and don't even get me started on romantic relationships). We owe it to one another, now more than ever, to be kind to other women, to hold space and empathy for one another, and to embrace whatever drama the patriarchy may try to stir up, and flip it on its head.

A technique I've found to be helpful here is practicing radical honesty with myself about my own feelings. When you really sit with your emotions toward other women, it becomes a lot easier to recognize the internalized misogyny that is driving your reactions and responses. If I saw a woman I didn't know, but felt disdain toward for no reason, I started to ask myself: *Is she* actually *a bad person? Or am I just being a hater? And if I am, why?* This kind of thinking really changed the game for me, because it allowed me the space to not only sit with my feelings, but also confront my prejudiced thoughts. Remember, it's not only a symptom but a goal of the patriarchy to pit women against one another. Modifying my thought patterns gave me autonomy and allowed me to consider if I was going to give in to this misogynistic and unproductive attitude toward women who have done nothing to me, or if I was going to decide for myself how I viewed them.

It not only opened my eyes to the biased beliefs I subconsciously held, but also opened my heart to so many different relationships and to the ability to build a community with many amazing women. If I had let that sour, misogynistic attitude that was imposed on me for so long limit my capacity to let other women in with an open heart and an open mind, I wouldn't have the many wonderful bad-bitch girlfriends I have today. So if you're a woman/femme reading this now, and you struggle with internalized biases, I want you to know that you aren't alone in that journey or in holding those biases. But there is always time to fix them by confronting them head-on.

Myth 4: You Can Fix Him

I wanna stress and emphasize this before we get into it: I am not a relationship therapist. I'm no relationship expert. Babe, I barely have any relationships in my past. All I have is real-world experience, a big mouth, and the utmost conviction that *most* women in this world could do MUCH better. So take that for what it's worth, bitch.

Now repeat after me: "No, I cannot fix him." And: "It is not my job to."

Your romantic relationship should not make you feel bad about yourself; have you questioning your passions, ambitions, or desires; or fill you with nerves about how your partner could react to something you did or said. You should never feel like you need to conceal information or keep secrets from your friends and family. You should be excited to see your person, and they should be fully accepting of who you are, as a complete, whole, and fulfilled person, with or without them by your side. They can obviously hold you to high standards, but they should not expect you to fundamentally change who you are for them. Being with them should be a reprieve from the other stresses in your day-to-day existence, not the main source of stress itself. If the person you're dating is filling you with anxiety, it's a sign that something isn't right. Your body is sending you a warning signal and that fight-or-flight trigger isn't going away. It's there for a reason.

You're not alone. It's *normal* to go through the experience of being with the wrong person. It sucks. But if you're honest about it, the experience can offer an intense period of personal growth when you uncover who you are and how you actually want to be treated within the context of a romantic partnership. However, if you're not careful around the wrong men, you can end up in a bad place, with depleted confidence and a drained sense of self. The core belief at the center of this display of martyrdom is the conviction that he will *change*. That who he is at his worst isn't actually who he is at all. That behavior can be corrected, and you alone will be the one to fix him. And even beyond that: it's your *job* to fix him, no matter the collateral damage (and every time, that ends up being you).

It's never okay to lose yourself in another person like this. It's an impulse that, once again, feeds into the mindset of scarce opportunities for women. You have to keep the faith that the right person for you is out there. Don't lose sight of the life you actually want, or the steps that you need to take to better yourself on an emotional and spiritual level to prepare for the right person to enter into it. Keep your head up and don't be shy about calling out red flags early on in your relationship. Resist the urge to look the other way when you see things you don't like, or to justify behaviors of his that don't make you feel good. Turn to close friends and trusted ears to voice concerns, and actually listen to them. You stand a higher chance of holding yourself accountable for your feelings when you don't ignore them, so don't be shy about making them known to those around you.

And if you're on the outside witnessing a friend going through a relationship like this, I know it might be hard to know what your role is, but I do believe you have a responsibility to say something, gently but firmly, if you see them losing themselves or behaving in a way that concerns you. Friends look out for friends, even if that means saving them from themselves.

In so many ways, male partners who make you feel this way on a consistent and aggressive basis can also turn from bad behavior to good behavior on a dime. When it's good, it's like being in a fairy tale. There's flattery, praise, and time spent together, intense talks about your future, maybe a showering of gifts. But there is *always* a tipping point. Suddenly, his love for you gets turned on its head and pointed back to his own insecurities, e.g., that you don't love him *nearly as much* as he loves you. Or if you *really* loved him you wouldn't dress that way and you wouldn't go out without him. He's just trying to *protect* you, and how can he do that if he doesn't control every aspect of your autonomy? He would do anything for you, he doesn't need anyone else on this earth other than you, and all he cares about is the two of you being together. Is it such a crime to simply recognize that you have a lot more going for you? Men like this don't care. It's only once you're asked to get on his level, too, that the praise and affection suddenly reveal themselves as a trap. Once he's flipped, he only wants you to feel guilty and to fall on your sword. The patriarchy has been conditioning women their entire lives to prioritize other people's feelings and comfort over their own, but you cannot give in.

It only takes one vicious fight with someone to know that it will happen again and again and again. Sure, there are interpersonal aspects to relationships such as communication styles that can be worked on, but they do not include punching walls or verbal abuse. They do not include shrinking yourself down to make him "feel like a man." They do not include justifying his actions that make you feel uncomfortable. Not every man is terrible; obviously we know this. But some are lost, some have been jumping from relationship to relationship their entire lives, and some are still dealing with internalized biases that they refuse to work on. That doesn't mean that you have to sacrifice your happiness for their love. That doesn't mean it's your responsibility to heal them. That's not how relationships are supposed to work. You deserve someone who gives you all the love and respect you want or desire from a romantic relationship, and that person should know that you refuse to settle for less.

When he tells you who he is, believe him the first time. I don't worry about you holding space for a partner. I worry about your partner holding space for you! Not just putting you on a pedestal and letting you believe you're better than everyone else. I'm talking about space to honor your individuality and independence, space to celebrate who you *truly* are. I want someone to see you the way you deserve to be seen. A true understanding and appreciation of who you are.

You should never be the only person with respect for the other in a relationship overall, but especially when there's turmoil. Arguing and fighting are two different things. Arguing with your partner is healthy. It means you're trying to communicate an emotion or something you're going through, but aren't yet feeling heard or understood. It's inevitable that you will argue with someone you spend so much time with (honestly, if you're not, I'm worried for you and that you're not speaking up enough). Fighting, however, is different from arguing. Fighting is not productive or healthy. It's just saying mean shit to each other, hyped up on emotion and adrenaline. It's not moving your communication forward, and *no one* is being healed—it's just trying to one-up each other, and that creates stress and walls between you and your partner. When you fight, you're not thinking logically, you're reacting off of emotion and have a higher risk of saying things that you don't mean and can't take back. And a lot of fighting can not only affect your overall mental well-being, but also has the potential to create tears in the foundation of your relationship with each other.

I know there are couples out there who have overcome an extraordinary amount together in their lives, and I'm not trying to suggest that you're perfect and that you deserve someone perfect, too, but I will say that the higher your standards walking into a partnership, the better you will fare in standing your ground and asserting yourself. At the very least, you will be unafraid to walk away at the moment your gut tells you it's simply gone too far.

Love, adoration, and having someone care so deeply about you shouldn't hurt. And it should never *have* to hurt in order for you to perceive it to be real. I think that far too often, people believe love needs to come with pain in order to be real. They think to themselves, *Well, nobody's perfect. And no relationship is perfect.* I also think it's possible that sometimes you may consider love and pain as a package deal because you may be afraid to pursue something that *seems* too good to be true. If you're someone who is afraid of committing to one person and worried when someone shows you the love you *actually* deserve, you may tend to gravitate toward someone who you know, deep down, is going to hurt you.

The mentality of *I know they make me feel like shit, but they're a shitty person, so I kind of figured they would do that* helps alleviate the chances of you *actually* committing to someone and getting hurt or suffering loss. And while I empathize with this very valid and common fear, I also know: not taking a leap of faith eliminates risk and possibility equally. C. S. Lewis said in *The Four Loves*, "To love at all is to be vulnerable. Love anything, and your heart will certainly be wrung and possibly be broken. If you want to make sure of keeping it intact, you must give your heart to no one, not even to an animal." This is no way to live. If this is you, too, don't be afraid to pursue someone who is willing to give you the love and support you want. You do deserve it! Ask yourself: *Why do I think relationships need to hurt in order to feel valid and tangible?* It's probably true that all love comes with some degree of turmoil, but you should never think you need to suffer alone in order to earn someone's love for you.

Words are so much more important than you think they are. Men who don't understand the difference between trying to communicate an emotion and just being mean love to blur lines and conflate the two, intentionally or not. They'll use the anger as an excuse and ask for forgiveness because they didn't *actually* mean what they said. But once the damage is done, there is no going back. Women are socially conditioned to accept apologies and overlook bad behavior, but at what cost? You don't need to forgive a person just because they asked you to and they would like for you to be ready to move on. Don't be so quick to grant exemption. Guard your personhood at all costs, because at the end of the day, you need to be looking out for yourself, *especially* when you're inside a relationship with another human being. When you look in the mirror, *that* is the person you are stuck with, day in, day out, for the rest of your life. And that *is* the most important relationship in your life, no matter what.

The irony is, a lot of women stay in these less-than-ideal relationships precisely because of the manipulative messaging they've been fed by the patriarchy their whole lives—the fear of being the undatable woman who ends up alone, the worry that there aren't that many chances to fall in love or experience deep human connection, and the belief that they're competing against other women for every opportunity in life. The examples in this chapter are just a small sampling, but there are endless misogynistic myths that continue to influence our world. My hope is that by beginning to call some of them out, you'll feel empowered to identify other commonly held misconceptions. You'll experience a euphoric sense of autonomy, deciding once and for all that you are worth taking care of. You deserve it.

That's what I want for you, and I know you'll get it. You just have to be willing to hold out for it. Never let a mediocre man who heavily weighs the opinions of other men when it comes to how he chooses to love you convince you that that is normal. And even more than that, don't let him convince you that turning on your fellow women is necessary in order to get a man. Letting him rob you of a life filled with the warmth of women is a painful and lonely experience. We can only survive if we have one another. From being told what is "ladylike" and how we are supposed to groom our own bodies, to unfounded criticisms we receive for being overly emotional and unpredictable, to the assertion that men are more even-tempered and naturally qualified for leadership positions, the list goes on.

It is overwhelming when we actually stop and consider all of the misogyny that continues to pervade society today. No one should attempt to reflect on it in isolation. We must listen to one another's experiences so we can ask questions, think critically, and decide for ourselves what is reality, and what the patriarchy has conveniently taught us to believe and expects us to follow along with, no questions asked.

These aren't just insensitive comments we hear once or twice a year from right-wing family members at Thanksgiving dinner. These are beliefs each one of us is forced to endure on a *daily* basis, and all of this messaging has a compounding effect, weighing heavier on our self-worth with each passing year on this earth. That is, until we reach the point when we are ready to begin the process of decentering men from our core beliefs. To get there, we have to understand the difference between how our society expects men and women to derive their sense of self in this world, and stay dogged in our conviction that we are so much more than what men expect us to be. We deserve to take up space, to speak our minds, to know we hold value beyond what the male gaze deems worthy of praise. Recognizing these misogynistic trappings as efforts to hold us back is a key first step in the journey toward decentering men from our individual journeys through life.

6

I'D RATHER DIE ALONE

Given all the overt and subtle ways that the patriarchy fucks with us, on both individual and structural levels, I dream of the day women and femmes decide we're all fully over this shit and that we're opting out. Although it isn't our fault that the system exists, living in direct opposition to it by refusing to participate is something I wish for all of us.

Fantasies aside, there is immense power in reaching the level of give-no-fucks that I personally have arrived at. By that I mean I've reached a place in my life where I have no problem with the idea of dying alone. There are no ifs, ands, or buts about it. It's true that I have already found the love of my life and the perfect partner for me in Pili, but I have made peace with the fact that if, for some reason, he did not exist, I would gladly and unapologetically brave this terrifying world with no romantic partner. I know you might be thinking that it's easy for me to say that since I *do* have Pili, but I assure you that this was a conclusion I came to long before he and I started dating. I actually fully credit my reaching this mindset for why the universe decided to send me Pili when and how it did.

Women who decide to live alone are often looked down on because men assume that we would only come to that conclusion for superficial reasons, like being spurned or rejected, unlike men, who can remain bachelors their whole lives as they're cheered on for not letting a woman tie them down. First of all, anyone's experience coming of age in this fucked-up patriarchal world *should* convince them that being alone is better than being with a subpar man. There is no "negative" experience required for women to see the potential of an awful man, especially when most times these experiences are inflicted on us against our will. Second of all, I don't see those reasons—being rejected within a cis-hetero patriarchal system that values whiteness and thinness can be a monumentally devastating experience—as superficial, but I know that's how they are perceived by men.

For every woman who voluntarily remains single, there is judgment surrounding that choice to stand alone in life and be happy about it. It's never treated as an autonomous decision, nor do people believe that we can be not only happy alone, but ecstatic and thriving. We're never allowed to *decide* of our own free will that being alone is better for us than being with someone who isn't enough. No one wants to believe that narrative. Only the one in which we're *forced* to make that choice . . . because a man hurt us so deeply, or no one would have us, or we aren't "marriage material." Men have to believe that a woman can only want to live alone if she has no other option. Any possibility of us having the agency to decide whether or not we want to be truly and happily alone scares them.

For me personally, I didn't arrive at this conclusion from a place of perceived lack or negativity. On the contrary, it was only when I fully came into my power as an independent woman that I truly began to embrace the prospect of dying alone. Because part of the work of knowing who you are is knowing what you can offer. And I was certain that what I was willing to give a male partner was nothing short of exceptional, and that I was more than capable of loving and giving that love to anyone who willingly entered a relationship with me. In fact, I felt the way that I did *because* I felt such a deep conviction that I was way more than enough, and I truly believed, in my heart of hearts, that no man I had ever met actually deserved what I had to offer him. It made no sense to chase after a subpar man out of loneliness, when there is actually nothing more lonely than living life in an emotionally unbalanced relationship. Rather than let that chip away at my self-esteem and self-worth, I choose to protect my own time, space, and energy, and fully live the way I want to live.

When it finally clicked, this was the most freeing realization that I'd ever made. That I was more than enough not only for someone else . . . but for myself alone as well. As Beyoncé says, "I'm gon' be my own best friend." And I will— I'd rather be my own best friend, other half, and best person I know than be met with subpar care and affection from a man who refuses to work on himself. The most amazing thing about this epiphany is that once you get there, there's no going back. The fear of missing out on a partner completely dissipates, and you're left feeling not only confident, but free. My complete acceptance of—even joy in—the thought of dying alone has not only served as the very foundation of my self-confidence, but also paradoxically led me to find an amazing male partner who truly loves and respects me.

But before I get ahead of myself, let me back up and tell you how I finally learned to stop worrying and embrace the idea of dying alone.

Throughout college, the running joke in my friend group was that I was way too picky. Even then, I already had a zero-tolerance policy for male bullshit, which meant that I ruled out guys after the smallest misstep, from making up a word right after he got done telling me how smart he was, to littering in front of me. I dated here and there during my time in college, but I never pursued anything serious because nothing ever felt . . . *right.* For most of school I was caught in a melancholy daze of never wanting to bring *any* of the dudes I was dating around my friends or family. Partially because it was hard to be serious about these guys who were so unserious, and if I wasn't serious about them, there was no way I was letting them have access to my inner circle. Even for the guys who weren't outright horrible and made it past the initial assessment, there was always something missing, and no matter what, I would always find a reason to bail. My friends would laugh about it all the time, but as I neared college graduation without ever having had a long-term, let alone meaningful, relationship, there would be moments when I started to wonder if maybe they were right. Maybe I *was* too picky.

I've always been the "mom" of my friend group. If you're sick, I *am* the annoying friend texting you ten times asking if you need delivery, if you've made a doctor's appointment, if you've turned off the work email and gotten some rest yet. Basically, I take care of everybody in the way I know how to from growing up with my mom. You could say it became my friendship love language: sticking up for my friends and gassing them up. Making sure they were aware of how much better they deserved than the shitty dudes we would randomly meet or go to school with. I never missed an opportunity to remind them that these guys sucked ass and would never be good enough for them, even if they *seemed* okay right now.

I also was already on my beat as crusader for other women and femmes around me at this time, having seen the ominous dangers ever present in what we loosely define as "college hookup culture." I took care of my friends when we went out and they were trying to drink and have fun. We could never be too careful when it came to having "normal college experiences," quote-unquote, because as women, we were vulnerable. We had to have our heads on a swivel at all times. College years promise young men the time of their lives playing, partying, and objectifying women for their own pleasure. We girls were just trying to have a good time, too, believing we were also entitled to that, but coexisting among men never really makes that an easy journey, does it? We had to be cautious, but not too much. Be fun, but not too much. Be hot, but not too much. And despite that impossible balancing act, sometimes it still wasn't enough to protect the women I love from getting harmed by men.

All I could do was comfort them as best I could when men inflicted every kind of violence on them, both physical and emotional, and try to build them back up in the aftermath. Because that's the hallmark of being a woman in this world. Soldiering on even when the unfathomable happens to you . . . because the world doesn't give you a chance to patch yourself up. That's where I always saw, and continue to see, myself coming in. If no one is going to remind you that you're worth more than all of these awful men combined, I will.

Even if situations didn't escalate to violence, there was always plenty of other shitty male behavior to contend with. I spent so much of my college life playing watchdog for all my friends, going over to their apartments and kicking guys out who'd try to freeload or miss major hints that it was time to leave. I'd stay alert at the bar and keep my eyes on everyone's glasses, whether they were girls I knew or not. And I always made sure my ride home came last, so I could ensure that no one was left behind or stuck in a situation that could turn out to be unsafe in my absence.

Surrounded as I was by male behavior like that, dating did not look to be in the cards for me. But in my last year of college, I started seeing someone.

I met him randomly on the beach with a group of friends and we spent the entire day together just talking and getting to know each other. Maybe it was because he was in his late twenties and seemed to be more mature than the average man I might date, but I was drawn to him. For someone who had only dated *very* casually and occasionally for the last three years, I was just as surprised as my friends were by the timing. Who knows, maybe I was getting soft with graduation ahead. But even so, from the jump, I could tell this guy was a little more serious than the ones I knew at school. He always wanted to see me and was proactive about initiating texts and making plans. Every time I'd get a text from him with an actual suggestion for a date, I'd be pleasantly surprised (which is such an ick if you think about it, because why is that exciting? The bar is in hell).

But then the problems started. I began to notice that whenever *I* attempted to make plans, he would always say no. He'd continue to ask me out for dates, but they'd always be on his schedule, and he'd always have an excuse ready for why he couldn't meet me when I asked him to. Even my friends agreed that this was most likely a red flag, but for some reason I chose to ignore it. I like to think this was my one major ignoring-gigantic-red-flag experience. It's a canon event for those of us who are, unfortunately, attracted to men, and I know you've been there, too, bitch. He was attractive, attentive, and up front about his interest, so I ignored the signs for a while, but he just kept being shady, which is so on brand for awful men, isn't it?

After a couple of weeks of his evasive behavior, with the help of my friends, I decided he was either (a) ashamed of me or (b) hiding something (and whatever that was it was definitely not going to be good news for me). So I decided that I would start telling *him* no each time he hit me up, too.

He caught on quickly and immediately changed his tune,

asking to come see me to explain. He drove over to my house, so I decided to give him one last chance. If he wanted to talk we could talk, but that would be it and then he would leave.

Big mistake.

Extremely long story short: I was the other woman. This man was living a double life and entangled me in his bullshit web of lies. After he relayed the details to "explain," my immediate response was *Wow, okay, mazel tov, but I'm fucking out.* Was he out of his goddamn mind? Begone, demon! But of course, because he's an awful person, he continued to ride the apology train, while stopping at every single excuse station. *It doesn't matter. I don't love her. Who cares? I've never felt this way about anyone before. I need you.* Boy, if you don't go to hell IMMEDIATELY.

After I conducted an exorcism on my house to dispel it of the bad spirits his lying, adulterous ass clouded my domicile with, he left. And of course, like they always do, he kept reaching out. He called me all the time, would blow up my phone and try to "check in," etc. It went on like this well into the following semester. When spring break rolled around, I went on vacation with my family and I got a call from my landlord. There was a drunk guy outside the house banging on my front door and shouting for me, blabbering on about how he missed me and was sorry. I told y'all he was a demon! I was so angry and genuinely confused. All of his shenanigans aside, we'd been "dating," if you could even call it that, for a couple of months, *maybe.* Even if he was the first guy I'd tolerated for longer than a few weeks, we weren't nearly serious enough to warrant this kind of behavior.

For some reason, I kinda felt sorry for the guy. When I

arrived back in Hawai'i from vacation, he asked to come over *again* because he wanted to talk *again*, and because I was in my eyes-wide-shut era, I let him come over just to talk. Once he got there, he just unloaded on me, trauma dumping about his relationship (you know, the one I was unknowingly intruding on) and explaining over and over how he still had feelings for me and how he "needed" me—and I realized, as he was sitting there blubbering in his own self-pity bubble, that he gave me the biggest ick. I was truly disgusted at the sight of him just sitting there, crying about how unfair the world was to him; meanwhile, he's actively trying to ruin the lives of two different women. The whole time he was yapping on and on, I just kept thinking to myself, *Men disgust me and this is karma for choosing to ignore the red flags.*

At this point, I was completely checked out of whatever it was we once had going on romantically, but he just couldn't let me go for some reason. He kept popping back into my life over and over again. I figured he clearly had lost his mind if he thought I was the girl to fuck with, and he would eventually stop reaching out to me. But he didn't. And at this point, I was getting angry every time I heard from him. This man was living like Jason Bourne in order to have two relationships on the same tiny island and he wanted me to feel bad . . . why? Because I couldn't be manipulated to stay once I found out he was a piece of shit? Eat a dick, sir.

So finally I decided to cut him off completely by ignoring him. I was not going to answer any more texts or pick up any more calls. I was blocking him once and for all. It seemed like he got the hint, and the communication died off.

Fast-forward a couple of months. I'm in my last few weeks

of school, about to graduate, studying for finals, when I get a call. It's around two in the morning from a number I don't know with a Honolulu area code. I thought it might be a family emergency, so I picked it up. On the other end was a woman's voice.

"Is this Drew?"

"Yeah . . . Who's this?"

"Do you know [REDACTED]?"

"Yeah . . . why? Who's this?"

She broke down crying. ". . . I fucking knew it. I literally knew it." I was so confused at first, but once she started sobbing on the phone, I knew. This was clearly the woman who had been in his life before me. I just couldn't tell if she was calling me to yell at me or what. She didn't seem mad, but she couldn't stop sobbing as she told me what had happened.

Turns out, there was much more to this story that I didn't even know. As she cried and shared their entire history with me, I just listened in disbelief. As much as I already believed he was capable of being awful, I could not have predicted just *how* awful. So I listened. I listened as she confided in me how she had been feeling, how she found out, the measures she went to to try and keep him from cheating, and so much more. And, look, it's not my place to air someone else's dirty laundry, especially that of another woman who's been to hell and back for a dumbass bitch of a man, but I promise you, the details were awful. At this point, any semblance of pity I might have had for him was incinerated. As much as I hated how he'd made me a "mistress" against my will, all of my empathy was redirected toward her. I couldn't believe that someone with such little regard for women he allegedly cared about, and their feelings, wanted me to believe that he was "hurting." Yeah fucking right.

I reassured her that I'd had no idea she existed, let alone that they were actively in a relationship, and that the minute I found out I cut it off. I don't need to interfere in anyone else's committed relationship in order to get a date, and I wanted to make sure she heard that from me.

I'm not sure if that made her feel any better, but we then went on to talk for *hours*, and I did my best to convince her to leave him, because this woman's freedom felt far more important than anything else I could've been doing at the time. I told her, "We both deserve better! FUCK HIM!"

In the moment she was all in, and she said she was going to leave him. I have no idea if she followed through, but I do hope that she found peace and love. This was one of those times when someone was in need of empathy and support, especially from another woman. I hope that she felt validated and heard, even if it was just for a moment.

A few weeks go by, but sure enough, a text from him pops up on my phone. In what was probably the most manipulative message I've ever seen in my goddamn life, he wrote, *I just wanted to say I'm sorry that you got mixed up in this and I appreciate you telling her what she needed to hear. You're right: I have a lot to work on.* Bitch . . . you should've seen my face.

It took all the strength in my body not to write back, because I knew he was going to take any response from me as encouragement. That's how these men operate. But it didn't end there. He followed up with another text: *Drew, you're the greatest person in the world. Are you just going to ignore me forever?*

Yes . . . I absolutely was. And I did. Thankfully, we never spoke again after that (and not for lack of trying on his end, either). I respect myself too much to hold space for an almost-thirty-year-old man who consciously chose to cheat on his long-term partner. You can suck my dick instead, buddy.

Looking back, I think I struggled a bit with why I was ignoring so many signs in the beginning. I had just given that terrible man *way* more time on the fucking field than he deserved, even when I had benched other dudes for much, much less. At that moment I promised myself that I would *never* go through that again. As stupid as misogynistic men are, they have mastered the art of lying. I vowed I would never fall for a man's empty words again.

At first, it started as a joke: *With men like this, I'd rather die alone.* But the more I said it, the more I found power in that statement. Because it was true—I'd rather stay in and do something *I* want to do, or hang out with friends who actually like and respect me, than go on a date with some horrible man. After all, nothing makes you lose faith in long-term heterosexual romantic companionship more than the process of dating men.

So I get it when other women come to me with their struggles, because I've been there, too. Don't get me wrong, a bad bitch is still a bad bitch, regardless of how many times she doubts herself, but I think that's the most human feeling in the world: loneliness. It's totally normal to feel a longing for companionship and love, and to want to feel connection and closeness with a significant other. I think what I started to realize, and continue to repeat to myself even in those moments of doubt, is that there's a big difference between being lonely and being alone. Loneliness is not permanent—it's an emotion. And emotions are like waves: they ebb and flow, they come and they go. So as quickly as this feeling came, it could easily be washed away if I reminded myself: *I am not lonely, I am alone. And there's nothing wrong with that.*

Dying alone (without a romantic partner) is very different from dying lonely. If anything, it's usually the opposite—when you don't have a terrible man by your side, you can form deeply intentional bonds with the friends and family you surround yourself with instead. You already know that I have an amazing family and that I am all about the girls, but the reason I love doing what I do is how many different kinds of people it brings me in contact with, of all genders, races, and backgrounds. Befriending people from all walks of life and educating yourself past your own sociological bubble is the only way to widen a limited worldview, and inherently makes you a better person and ally along the way. It's made me open and receptive, and forced me to be introspective. There's a beauty in unlearning all the ways patriarchy has held you down and prevented you from being happy for other women. I truly believe maintaining a strong friend circle of women, femmes, and anyone else who isn't a cis-het straight man is necessary to mentally and emotionally thrive in this world at any age.

As humans, we naturally crave connection. Saying you'd rather die alone isn't about whether you actually do. It's about the shift in mindset to know that you could. Remember: nothing scares a man more than a woman who knows she does not need him.

When I looked around, I could see what an amazing circle of friends and wonderful family I had, all of whom loved me unconditionally. And if I looked in the mirror, I could remind myself that I loved the woman standing before me more than any man ever could. That should be enough. You should never have to outsource the foundation of your self-love. It was always meant to come from within. And because no one can take care of and love me like I love myself, if it came down to it, I could do it alone. I could die alone for all I care, because that's what I would rather do than give my love to someone undeserving. I repeated this mantra to myself over and over again, until I started to believe it. And once I did, the universe decided to change course for me and direct me to my soulmate (of fucking course it did). The minute you give up on trying to find love, it'll find a way to deliver it to you.

Dating my boyfriend, Pili, was not something I ever planned on happening. In fact I'm just as shocked as the men who hate me that we ended up together. Not because I think he's too good for me (please), but because it wasn't something that seemed to be in the cards for us. We went to high school together and were friends all throughout, but never pursued each other romantically. To give you a sense of what that looked like, he was the only Samoan guy at our school, which meant *all* of the other Samoan girls would fawn over him. That sort of power imbalance has always been a major turnoff for me. Plus, it wasn't just the Samoan girls who were interested, it was *most* girls, period. Back then, Pili had this Justin Bieber haircut that he would flat-iron into the perfect swoosh.

What can I say? It was the early 2010s, and this was Southern California, but even so, it's fair to assume he hadn't come into his own yet, rocking a white-boy teenybopper hairstyle that looked so wrong on a six-foot-four football player. It made me uneasy, probably because I recognized his insecurity. If I'm being honest, it also made me nervous about my own (not about my haircut).

Now when we look back, we laugh because we admit that we both found each other attractive and recognized that, but both thought that it would never work. He was confident; I was confident. He was an athlete; so was I. He was charming; so was I. He was a know-it-all . . . and so was I. It was almost like we both knew that if we pursued each other it could be great, but we didn't want to find out if it was terrible, either. So we didn't. We were never anything more than pals. He even asked me to the prom our senior year and I said no. That's how stubborn I am. We remained friends, went to college, and got lunch like old coworkers once in a while. We never thought anything would come out of our very flippant friendship. But after I graduated from college and moved home, something changed.

I was doing everything in my power to stay in Hawai'i. I should have had more than enough professional experience to get a job there, and I had roots planted in the community, but none of my sports journalism leads panned out. I was so confused as to how that could possibly happen—I was confident in my hireability and ready to hit the ground running toward my professional goals after graduation—but now I know why: the universe was pushing me home for a reason. Pili reached out multiple times after I got back to California, but

I ignored him (for reasons that are silly, but essentially he had flaked on me one too many times when we were trying to hang out as friends and I was over it). After many shitty excuses, I couldn't put up with his flakiness any longer, so I decided I didn't need to see him anymore. The joke was clearly on me, bitch. The thing about Pili is he doesn't do anything he doesn't want to do. So the fact that he continued to reach out to ask me to spend time together was very out of character for him, especially the version of him I remembered from high school. And he knew that I was ignoring him for blowing me off, so when he reached out to me the fourth time, he said, *I know you're mad at me and I don't blame you. Please let me make it up to you. If you aren't interested, I'll leave you alone. I promise.*

And for some reason this message really stuck out to me. I remember showing it to my mom and she told me, "He sounds really sorry. You should hang out. And if he sucks, then at least you get a free meal and then you never have to talk to him again." The logic sounded bulletproof to me, so I agreed to hang out. He seemed excited when I reached back out, and planned a whole day for us and told me he would pick me up at a very specific time. I was taken aback by his proactive nature, but I agreed.

First thing I noticed when he came by my house that day was his hair. It was grown out, long, and piled on top of his head so I could see his undercut. Even my dad noticed. He said, "He looks really good." Now, if you're thinking to yourself, *Drew, did you really have a change of heart about Pili just over his hair?*, let me remind you that, one: I am simply a woman—what do you want from me? And, two: I hadn't seen him in person in close to three years, I didn't remember how handsome he was, and I don't want to talk about it. The person who showed up that afternoon was not the immature teenager I remembered; he was a grown, evolved man. Someone who knew what he wanted and didn't have to hesitate or think twice before deciding to go after it. And even after all this time, he knew having me in his life was one of those nonnegotiables.

We caught up that afternoon over lunch, and in our conversation, I realized just how much he'd matured since I'd last seen him. He was passionate about what he'd finished studying at school in his sociology major and had academic language now for describing so much of the experience we shared. For example, he was the one who taught me a metaphor he'd learned in school to describe intersectionality—something I very much saw and was aware of, but never had the words to articulate. He described it for me in terms of a classroom. The people in the first row come from the strongest points of privilege, e.g., white cis men, ahead of rows occupied by people with decreasing amounts of opportunity as it comes to the intersection of their gender identity, sexuality, race, class, whether or not they're able-bodied, etc., with the very least privileged standing at the back of the class. So if you sit in the very front, you don't think oppression exists, because you can't see it. It's up to the people at the front of the classroom to acknowledge their point of privilege and make a concerted effort to turn around and look back.

And I know . . . Pili introducing *me* to feminist theory? And not in a mansplaining way, but one that provided an intelligent and clear framework for me to think about a concept that had formerly been abstract? Ew, I love it so much it makes me sick. Why? This understanding of intersectional feminism became an incredibly important framework for my beliefs moving forward. One I never lost sight of as I continued to repair my relationship with my sister and learn about her experiences and perspective as a queer person. And one I always try my best to carry with me into every single human interaction.

We took it slow over the next few months, just getting to know each other again, but I think we both understood from that day forward where this was going. Fast-forward almost six years later, and here we are, madly in love with each other and building a life together. Pili had never reached out to someone so many times and gotten no response, and when I asked him why he did that with me, he told me that something kept telling him he would regret it for the rest of his life if he didn't patch up our relationship. He knows now that it was because he was supposed to fall in love with me (and he brags all the time about how he knew before I did).

I think the universe has a really funny way of giving us what we want, not when we want it, but when we're ready to receive it. And I know now with the utmost confidence that I found my person because I was ready to. My self-confidence was at a point where, with or without a partner, I was going to be okay. I was going to live a long, fulfilling, and beautiful life regardless of my relationship status, and because I'd arrived at that state of mind, I was finally ready to be with my soulmate. I genuinely believe that was the plan for me all along when it came to romantic partnership.

Pili says that one of the reasons he knew he loved me was because he could tell that I didn't need him. I didn't *need* him to be with me to know my worth or be happy. I *allowed* him to be in my life because I loved him so much. I knew he wouldn't make my entire life, he would only enhance it, and the feeling was mutual. Pili is someone who really sees me for who I am, not what I'm perceived to be. He was the first person in my life to understand the person who I've always wanted to be, and strive to become every day. He makes me want to be the best version of myself, and vice versa, and that's a beautiful feeling. Every day I feel so incredibly grateful to have someone who celebrates every part of me (even my big personality, which scares away lesser men).

He is my equal in every way, as I am his. But what I want all of you to know and trust is that no matter how much I celebrate our love for each other, I'm never going to allow his love for me to outgrow or replace the love I have for myself. There is absolutely no one in this world worth letting go of your self-love for, and he is no exception to this rule. I believe that great relationships simply parallel the relationships those individual participants should have with themselves. First, you have to believe that you're worth it, and the right person will come at a time when you are not only ready, but prepared on a mental, spiritual, and emotional level.

When you grow up in a patriarchal society, men are always at the center, and you have to rip them out root and stem if you ever want to stop internalized misogynistic beliefs from growing inside you. It's damn near impossible to culti-vate unbreakable self-love when you still hold these beliefs in your heart. They are only holding you back. Without the anxiety of possibly ending up with a mediocre man, which often leads us to accept less than we deserve, you'll find that you'll be more free to discover yourself and invest in friendships that matter, all on the path to becoming more fulfilled and finally at peace with your life exactly as it is and exactly how you want it.

For me, it was my college friends who made me realize just how incredibly nuanced, caring, and expansive female friendship could be, especially compared to the friendships I had cultivated with men. Women are so intentional in the relationships they build with one another. The love, strength, and encouragement we are capable of giving one another when competition and internalized misogyny cease to disrupt the energetic flow between us are truly magical.

It was so important for me to find inspiring women outside of my family during my college years away from home. My mom would tell me all the time how powerful I was and how important I was going to be in the world, which provided me with an incredible foundation of self-confidence, but receiving validation not only from people related to you but from your peers as well is an incredible feeling. And as my circle grew and I received that same level of validation from other women I admired, that experience empowered and encouraged me to truly show up and make my presence known to the world. Their friendship has made me the person I am today. They truly were the ones who completed the process of ripping me out of a male-centered mentality and allowed me to replant my roots in a foundation of love, community, and support.

Don't think of dying alone as something to fear. It should

merely be an option you'll have unlocked once you've finally realized that you are worth all of the love and respect you have to offer in this world. An unworthy man is never going to offer you that, and you don't need to be with one simply because you're afraid of being alone. It's empowering to know that you can, and will (if need be), brave this life as a free agent surrounded by people who really love you instead of with a man who doesn't give a damn.

You deserve to be a priority. How can you prioritize another person in a romantic relationship before first prioritizing your own thoughts, feelings, and ambitions? You should always love yourself enough to hold out for the best, and not let the voice of the patriarchy convince you otherwise. Settling is a tool crafted by the worst men in the world, used solely to clip your wings. They want to take you down a peg so you don't realize just how incredibly special you are, because if you did, you know what that would mean? That these men would end up being the ones dying alone, involuntarily (as they should).

Learning how to love yourself—like, truly love yourself—is not easy. In fact, it might be one of the hardest things you'll ever have to do. But look, there's only one person you'll be with from the moment you are born until the moment you die—yourself. Give yourself a chance.

7

BODY NEUTRALITY

Let me preface this chapter by saying that I'm not an expert on any person's body but my own. The subject of our bodies and how much worth or value they hold is something women and femmes become aware of shockingly early on. We are conditioned to believe that there is a standard for what men will accept as attractive and that anything that falls outside of that standard is "bad" or "ugly."

This could be for a whole host of reasons because as we're all aware, the list of things women should be, have, and do is never-ending. Be thin but not too thin. Have big boobs but God forbid you show them off. Work on your body in the gym, but not too much, or that's "manly." Be funny, but never funnier than your man. Be outgoing, but not too much, otherwise you're too desperate for attention. The list goes on . . . and on . . . and on.

I get asked questions about dating a lot, but especially dating as a "bigger" girl. Many women and femmes who are attracted to men want to know how to navigate potential romance, and it's something I totally relate to, as I was never more acutely aware of my body and the way it was perceived or valued than I was once I started casually dating in my late teens and early twenties. The fact is, dating as a taller, thicker, brown woman is a way different experience from dating as a thin, white woman, which is the experience most often portrayed in popular media, from teen movies to reality television, and quickly I became aware of how differently my body, and in turn my thoughts and opinions, were being judged compared to women who fit within our culture's narrow beauty standards.

But the voice in your head that tells you you're "not worthy" of love or support from a romantic partner because your body/facial features do not fit into some arbitrary, Eurocentric box that bigoted men built is nothing more than internalized misogyny. It's a sinister tool that has been ingrained into our brains and belief systems. From the very first moment we gain sexual consciousness, we are led to understand that validation from men is a valuable social currency. As impossible as it may seem to accomplish, we must work tirelessly and consistently to expel this belief from our mindset. One of the biggest gaslights the patriarchy has normalized is that male validation is the be-all and end-all of life. That it's the one thing all women/femmes should strive toward, because what even is the point of life if you don't have a man giving you his stamp of approval?

Because, believe it or not, the inverse reaction to my size from guys who expressed their enthusiasm and excitement at having found a "thick" girl didn't make me feel any better. It made me feel like no matter who I was on the inside, no matter how multifaceted and intelligent I believed myself to be as a person, most men were incapable of seeing past my physical attributes. Which is a completely dehumanizing feeling. It's gross, feeling like you are nothing more than body parts, a mannequin to be ogled and objectified, and never an actual human being with thoughts and interiority, and unfortunately it is a feeling far too many of us have had to not only endure, but normalize. Personally, I wish we could just do away with commenting on other people's physical appearances altogether. Everyone deserves to feel comfortable in their own body, and love their body, even, but damn, do they make it hard for us to get there.

When I was still in high school, it seemed like there was a sudden uptick in targeted body positivity messaging. These were the early days of Instagram in 2012, when influencer culture was still in its infancy and the app taught us all what it looked like to wash over our photos with dozens of filters, all essentially serving the identical function of blurring imperfections and concealing reality to make life look a little more dreamlike. At the same time, though, the platform was making it possible for the body positivity movement, a once comparatively underground and grassroots initiative, to make its way to the masses. Via hashtags, of course, the two most popular of which were #bodypositive and #bodypositivity.

It was pretty cool to see in the early days of this movement

Black women and other women of color speak openly about their struggles with fatphobia and society's treatment of fat and plus-size women, and love their bodies openly and radically, despite what this racist, patriarchal world told them was "acceptable." However, as new as it was for social media to portray bodies that were not primarily thin, the movement gradually started to focus more on thin and midsize white women who hit a high bar of conventional beauty (regardless of their size) and professional models (for whom "plus-size" can describe anyone larger than a size six). In fact, a study that aimed to analyze whether the body positivity movement's two most popular hashtags actually upheld its initial goals found that the top posts linked to said hashtags did not actually stray from the hegemonic beauty standards of popular media at all, thus defeating the campaign's purpose.

As marketers and advertisers caught wind of this digital-age feminist rebranding, they were quick to adopt it for the purposes of selling their products. For decades these brands had enticed youths with pictures of impossibly thin, almost exclusively white all-American teenagers, prompting plenty of dressing room meltdowns from the adolescent girls who shopped at their stores, to make no mention of the plus-size clientele who were denied access outright because their sizes weren't even carried. Soon, brands began to boast about the wide range of sizes they carried or feature plus-size models in their campaigns, even if the models usually still conformed to white beauty standards. While this shift was long overdue, it quickly co-opted the original intention of the movement in order to sell us more things by brands that had made us feel excluded in the first place.

In the end, it seemed there may have been more harm done than good. What was once a space for those who live in the margins to not only see their body type represented, but also see people who looked like them being loved and happy and fulfilled in their lives, was now being washed away by women who have never truly known what it's like to be fat or plus-size in this violently vitriolic world.

And was it any surprise, really, that the lingerie and lotion brands wanted to participate in body positivity so long as it was trendy, but did little in the way of actually standing behind the bodies they were paying to represent them? For all its eventual faults and shortcomings, there was still plenty of research proving that access to positive affirmations of self-image would result in decreased anxiety and depression, especially among young women/femmes, but fatphobia persisted in articles and media coverage from both conservative news outlets and scientific journals alike that insisted the movement was encouraging unhealthy lifestyle habits—as if the editorialized ad campaigns offered any insight into the personal lives of its subjects whatsoever—and contributing to the obesity crisis. Advertisements for soda, candy, alcohol, and fast food? Forever and always completely fine. Advertisements for body lotion featuring plus-size models? They deemed this "irresponsible." Sadly, it comes as no surprise that our capitalistic society is terrified to embrace messaging that makes people feel seen and represented. After all, if they can't keep us striving, how can they keep us buying?

This reality always pulls me out of the urge to assign either negative *or* positive feelings to my body and instead work toward a state of body neutrality. Arriving at body neutrality is a journey that involves a tremendous amount of unpacking and unlearning. It's the belief that you can simply be at peace with your physical appearance. That your form is neither good nor bad, but a vessel that allows you to move and exist in the world. The only feeling you direct toward your body is gratefulness for what it does for you every day in keeping you alive. I prefer this approach to my own physical appearance because I want to be in a place where I appreciate what my body does for me and nothing more. I want to embody the idea that it's more than enough for my body to simply keep me happy and thriving.

The true freedom of body neutrality comes from the space it frees up in the mind. When we let go of the stress and consciousness surrounding what we look like, we make room for so much more. Why should we be expected to hold so much personal value in our looks and bodies when there are so many other dimensions to ourselves beyond what the outside looks like? This doesn't mean I don't take pride in my appearance, but what I'm working on believing and embodying the most in my body neutrality journey is the idea that the vessel is worthless if the contents inside are rotten.

And, look, I'm not here to tell you that you're not entitled to want to look a certain way. My nails definitely did not grow themselves, and I'm not afraid to put my consumer power to good use, either. What I am here to say, though, is that it's not okay for any of us to be spending a crippling amount of time or energy trying to cultivate the image that we think will positively affect how the patriarchy perceives our bodies. Terrible men don't deserve that and they never will.

The lens that we're first taught to look at ourselves through is usually a male lens, but the reality is that none of us are born with that understanding. As a child, I didn't register my physical form whatsoever. It did nothing for me other than keep me going. At recess, I played hard as shit getting sweaty and dirty with the other kids. I was already strong and athletic, and thanks to my general delusional demeanor, my initial, factory-setting body neutrality era actually lasted a lot longer than most people's do, which I didn't realize was such a gift until much later in life. I had no opinion about my weight or my looks, I just knew I was *the shit*. All of the attributes of myself that gave me confidence had nothing to do with my outer appearance. What a gift to not be weighed down by the opinions of men who will never affect my life in a positive way.

When I was close to puberty, the idea of my body being a factor in how I was valued began to creep in. I grew four inches in the summer between seventh and eighth grade, shooting from five foot four all the way up to five foot eight. Then one day, in the car on my way home from soccer practice, where I played on a team that was, aside from me, exclusively made up of small white girls, I mentioned to my mom in passing that some days I just wished I looked more like my best friend at the time (a sweet blonde, who, by the way, to this day is one of the nicest girls I've ever known). My mom responded right away, directly but gently. "I'm going to tell you something that sounds mean," she began, "but it's not. You are never gonna look like that."

That was my mom's style. She would always come down to our level and explain things in ways that were easy to digest. She never spoke to us as if we were stupid, and she never beat around the bush. It's one of the many reasons I think we are still so close to this day. This was the first time she and I had ever had a conversation about my body, and she was firm. "Not everyone should look the same. Everyone looks different because everyone comes from different families and the reality is that we're Samoan and you're a lot bigger than most girls. But that's not a bad thing. One day you're gonna love exactly how you look." She knew I had started to struggle with my height especially, because no other girls I knew were as tall, and it started to stick out more and more as I got older. At the time, I was confused by her forcing common sense into my deluded world, and I convinced myself she was wrong. Thinking out loud, I muttered, "I could probably lose weight." "Should you, though?" she asked. "Do you think you need to do that? Just because you can doesn't mean you should." *Ugh, whatever. You don't know!* I thought while subconsciously letting her sage wisdom move into the penthouse suite of my memory forever.

Looking back now, I am eternally grateful that we had this conversation. Hearing at such an impressionable age that my body does not look like other people's and there is nothing inherently wrong with that seems almost too simple to be groundbreaking, but it was. My body was not inherently bad because it didn't mirror those of my white counterparts, and that was okay. In fact, it was something to celebrate! I never forgot what that conversation did for me, mentally, all those years ago.

Then, during my freshman year of high school, I tore my ACL at a game and had to go to the hospital for major reconstructive surgery on my knee. The doctor took one look at my X-rays and delivered other good news (at least to me): my growth plates were pretty much closed . . . which meant I was done growing. Finally! At fourteen years old, standing five feet, nine inches tall (I grew one more inch before high school—what the fuck?), I was over the moon, ecstatic if you will. I even asked him to confirm for me, one more time, that I wasn't going to grow any more. Although I'd had conversations with my mom about celebrating the differences of my body, I was still a young high school girl, still vulnerable to the constant male validation and pick-me-isms swirling around me at that age, so when I heard that there was a chance I wasn't going to grow any taller, I was fired up. I wouldn't have to feel so insecure about being bigger than every boy who went to my school or towering over every girl I hung out with and played sports alongside. The doctor confirmed I was good. Never gonna grow again.

And guess what, bitch? I grew three more inches over the next three years. What a crock of shit. I was so bummed. At that age and period of my life, I was constantly reminded by boys—albeit insecure and small boys—who went to school with me that they *would* like me if I "wasn't so tall." Naturally, being the menace toward men I am, I would brush these comments off and be mean right back. I would claim how much I didn't care, because clearly they were struggling in the genetics department and I wasn't. But as a young woman surrounded by hormones and teenage high school drama, I'd be lying if I said it didn't bother me *at all*. I would wish all the time that I would stop growing, or even better, shrink, because society convinced me that since I wasn't fitting in the warped beauty standards box, no man would ever be attracted to me. *If I stop growing, then they'll catch up to me and it'll get easier* is what I told myself.

I didn't realize then even half of what I now know to be true. I may have been desperate to stop growing taller, but emotionally, there was a ton of growing left for me to do. Physically, mentally, and spiritually, there was absolutely no part of myself that I needed to stunt in order to better appeal to men.

The patriarchy's goal is to make you want to shrink and hide, both physically and emotionally. It wants you to be nervous about what will happen if you don't. *What if operating at 100 percent capacity negatively impacts people, and what if they resent that, and everyone resents you by proxy?* My entire adolescent experience was feeling like there was a part of me that I needed to hold back, that the full me would be too much and it would alienate everyone, but especially the men, around me. Because at the end of the day, it is always the men who are driving the narrative, dictating, *Well, I would like you better if you were . . . less.*

These feelings and anxieties really began to culminate for me at the beginning of my freshman year at the University of Hawai'i. College is such a perfect way to dip your toe into adulthood without really having to experience it, but I definitely noticed how men both perceived and treated the white girls in my friend group, and how different that was from the way they approached and talked to me. We were all super outgoing, vivacious girls, but I was never accepted or embraced as a potential romantic interest in the same way the white girls in my inner circle were. At first, I assumed that this had to be on me, so I did my best to tone it (whatever "it" was) down. I felt certain that my affinity for "too much" was the main reason I was not being treated the same as my white friends, and this belief began to weigh on me. I felt guilty about the part of myself that I was unsuccessfully holding back, and at the same time, I felt frustrated that I had to hold back in the first place. In reality, I was hurting myself infinitely more by suppressing who I really was in favor of how I thought I wanted to be perceived, especially by men. Unfortunately, this kind of social awareness haunts most women and femmes, who are forced on a daily basis to choose between themselves and male approval.

This frustrating double bind was never made more clear to me than during a conversation I had with a guy I knew, who happened to be a white man, on the topic of dating.

"What's your preference?" he asked.

"Looks-wise? Nothing, really," I replied. "Just someone who isn't horrible and is kind of funny is the baseline, though I'm not seeing many who can even meet that as of right now."

"Honestly, Drew," he began, "if I were to see you from the outside, and you had other friends with you that didn't look like you, I would more than likely approach them first because you intimidate me. You scare me a little bit. So I'm gonna go with what I know and what I'm comfortable with as opposed to running the risk of talking to you."

"Because I scare you?" I confirmed. ". . . okay."

Well, at least he was honest. He wasn't trying to be a dick, and as much as what he was saying pissed me off, I also felt weirdly validated hearing him convey the simple reality of the situation. Because it made me realize it was never about whether or not I was "too much" for these small, undeserving men. They all simply weren't enough *for me*. Men who were easily intimidated by my build, my personality, my laugh, ANY part of me that makes me uniquely myself, didn't have what it took. So what was I so worried about?

Of course, I couldn't ignore the way my race factored into this white man's assessment, as well as the fact that I am physically big as shit. But this was the first time I'd had someone admit to masculinizing me because of what I look like. And yet, I wasn't mad or upset about what he said. I felt nothing but indifference. Why? Because I wasn't attracted to him . . . *at all*. In fact, I didn't care about *his* opinion of me whatsoever.

After many more interactions like this, I eventually came to understand that it wasn't my problem, or my responsibility, to care about what mediocre men like or want. I began to fully grasp just how out of my own control this whole dating game was in some respects. This strange standard that was being forced on me was misogynistic not only to bigger women and femmes like me, but also to the many other women and femmes who guys were only interested in because they were smaller and assumed to be more vulnerable (which is a whole other layer of disgusting and evil). I would never be what they perceived as the "easy" choice for a man. So I decided to *intentionally* be the worst. If these guys were only going to judge us in terms of who's "approachable" and who's "intimidating," then I was gonna feel however the fuck I wanted to feel about my own body and looks overall. Because one thing about me? I'm not going to put all my worth and value in the incapable hands of a man who's easily "intimidated" by women who don't fit within a harmful and bigoted beauty standard. The stress I had put on myself to appeal to them was no longer viable and couldn't hurt me anymore.

At the root of our fear of being bigger (both physically and metaphorically) than men is the message that it will emasculate them, but emasculation is gravely misunderstood to be a woman's problem. In fact, I believe the idea that women can "emasculate" a man by being greater than him in any sense is a fallacy. You cannot make a man feel *less than* unless he first derives power from being stronger than you (in whatever capacity that is). The male gaze convinces us that we should value ourselves only through the narrow (and often racist/fatphobic/ableist) lens of what's attractive to men, when in reality, our bodies are individual works of art. We each encompass and hold such a palpable and divine energy that deserves to be celebrated on our own terms.

I'll be real here, I don't always *love* the way I look. And that's okay. Because even on the days I don't feel my most confident, or I feel that societal beauty standards are whooping my ass, I remind myself that I am more than what I look like. I ask myself, am I a good person? Am I making things that I am proud of? Am I taking care of the people I care about? And if the answer to all those questions is still yes, it helps center me. I am decidedly body neutral, and it's a part of myself I *still* have to work on every single day. I recite positive affirmations to myself over and over again, but most importantly, I make sure they have nothing to do with my looks. My decision to accept my perception of my own body in this way—neither hateful nor praiseworthy but in an in-between state that simply values it unconditionally while acknowledging my current good fortune in health and physical ability—allows me to remove my physical appearance from how I value myself altogether. This, in turn, has allowed me to focus on other areas of my life that are more impactful and important to me. Like being a good person, showing up for my community, and supporting those closest to me in every way I can. Oh, and not to mention running a successful brand and pursuing incredible business opportunities I thought I'd only ever dream about. Like writing this book.

So much of my self-confidence and empowerment begins with how I talk to myself, and it feels too risky to place my relationship to my own body at the center when there is such a small window for any of us to ever feel completely satisfied with our appearance. I don't want to be forty-five wishing I looked the way I did at thirty-five or twenty-five. No matter how much time, effort, and money you spend trying to achieve perfect curves and flawless skin, and chasing whatever beauty standard is currently trending, we will get older, and our bodies will change. And that's just the truth of it. I thought I had sealed the deal on living the rest of my life as a five-foot-nine woman when my doctor examined my growth plates at fourteen, but what do you know? I was destined to become the six-foot-tall bitch I am today all along. I still have no idea what the next year, let alone decade, has in store for the body I'm currently in. All I know is that I'm going to care for it, respect it, and be thankful for it, as best I can for as long as I can.

And, sure, I love good glam. I'm obsessed with clothes. And I go to the gym several times a week, too. But that's just physical and mental health maintenance, as far as I'm concerned. Ninety-nine percent of the time, my internal dialogue of what I say to myself and how I judge my character has nothing to do with my physical appearance. I strive to work toward body neutrality, and by focusing on that, I turn my attention away from what I look like, so I can instead be free to prioritize the desires within my heart and mind.

We all have the ability to do this for ourselves. I often think that people don't realize how important the words that they say to themselves in their own heads really are. Ask yourself, *What are the consistently positive things I say to myself when I look in the mirror every day?*

Whether you have no makeup on, or you're in a full beat; have landed a huge opportunity or made a mistake; made a great first impression or said something embarrassing—the biggest indicator of where you're at on your journey to self-acceptance is your relationship with yourself. Your words are so powerful—they can inspire and motivate you or completely derail you with or without any external forces already at play.

Beauty is subjective. It's not the same in the eyes of every person. Everyone has a different idea of what they find attractive, and what I find to be insane behavior is some people thinking they have the right to comment on what other people like, or determine who is or isn't attractive, when nobody asked them in the first place. Attraction is boundless, and it's more than skin-deep. When you find what you're looking for, you will find that person attractive around the clock, whether they've just rolled out of bed or are in a full face of makeup ahead of a night out. That's true, foundational love, baby. And the only people who think otherwise are the same people that think they're the president of the council of "who's good-looking and who isn't." Those people are nothing more than insecure, and insecure men especially love to look at couples who are happily together and point out, unprovoked, if they don't find one of the pair, and let's be real, it's usually the woman, to be conventionally "hot." They are in complete shock whenever they see a woman who they don't think conforms to the patriarchal ideal of attractiveness accepting romantic attention. It is, unfortunately, something that I encounter regularly as a person with an internet platform who just so happens to be in a long-term committed relationship with a man who looks like the alpha-male prototype.

Why do these mediocre men on the internet feel the need to comment on my appearance? Because they obsess over these standards set forth in the media as markers for who is entitled to give and receive physical intimacy and love. Believe it or not, if you are a woman or femme with your own brain that operates outside of the confined walls of male validation, and you stand up for yourself or others . . . chances are a misogynist is going to find you wildly unattractive. It's a tale as old as time. That's where the genesis of all the hate men feel toward me comes from: a deeply rooted and insecure confusion at an independent woman, who is loud and opinionated, being deeply in love with and loved by a man. And yes, my boyfriend is very attractive, objectively so, by our society's standards at least: tall, dark, and handsome. But that's not why I'm with him. I'm with him because he's kind, he cares about his mom and his brother, he looks after animals, and he is a true intersectional ally in every way. All of that is so much more important to me than him being hot . . . that's just a plus.

Women want so much more than giant Hercules pecs and a six-pack. These internet lunkheads think the key to landing women involves going to the gym seven days a week and eating a diet of protein powder and chicken breasts. Insisting you have to lift every single day, as opposed to working on what's inside, does nothing for women or their willingness to be attracted to you. All it does is distract these men from looking inward and doing the mental and emotional work necessary to become empathetic and interesting human beings.

Toxic masculinity also shames men who are attracted to people of all shapes and sizes into believing they need to adhere to what they believe other men find acceptable and attractive. They treat dating primarily as a way of elevating their status with other men, and this almost always encompasses ugly truths about racism, transphobia, and fatphobia. Misogynistic men love to worship one another, and tragically this activity can take precedence over finding any semblance of genuine connection with women, platonic or romantic. It's rotten, truly, but do you really want to waste your time with a guy who's only trying to date for the approval of his high-school-glory-days buddies? You can't respect someone, let alone try to date someone, who lacks the confidence to honor his own likes and dislikes (who instead interprets his ability to impress other men as having found success with women). The cruelest irony that men who hate me don't realize is that the patriarchy cages them, too. If they decided to fight alongside us, to unlearn and unpack all of this internalized misogyny, then they could also be free.

Recently, in dark corners of the internet where I'm called in to patrol by people who've sniffed something foul coming from the bigots inside, I found men who had given themselves a new moniker: the high-value man. This man is basically a misogynist who says he is committed to the masculine core evolutionary mandate.

These men have found one another on the internet and banded together, convinced that women/femmes discovering their autonomy somehow has equated to their version of being oppressed. I suppose this sort of ill-conceived, reactionary defense has been taking shape in some form since the dawn of the feminist movement, but when they start throwing out the counter-term "low-value woman" in relation to a woman who "doesn't deserve" a high-value man due to her independence or refusal to "submit," that's when I lose my shit. None of what they preach is rooted in any kind of fact or reality, and it's pseudoscience at best. Masculine, feminine, gender as we know it is a man-made invention, a by-product of colonization and religion, washed into our culture so that people coming up in society would be taught to hate themselves if they even dared to set foot outside of the very specifically curated gender binary that was imposed on all of us.

Capitalism shapes and feeds off of that ideology as well. When we're sad and our insecurities are being preyed upon, we're more likely to buy stuff we think will change our lives and make us feel better. But even the things we buy to comfort ourselves and make us feel better—our little treats, if you will—are susceptible to being gendered, which is why shopping for clothes is so often shown as a woman's guilty pleasure, while shopping for new tech is shown to be a man's.

Who are we performing for in society when we choose what to wear or how we style our hair or put on makeup? Our perceptions are deeply impacted by nuances of misogyny, from internalized fatphobia to slut shaming, that are important to recognize and flag for what they really are. There are countless opportunities to let harmful messaging in if we're not diligent about keeping patriarchal opinions out and constantly working on unlearning all of our internalized biases. The goal should never be to spend time, energy, and money on trying to fit into these narrow Eurocentric standards at the expense of celebrating every unique part of yourself. When you accept yourself, truly—and not in a hyperconfident and cocky way, but in a way that is a day-in-and-day-out commitment to treating yourself as worthy and deserving (because you are)—you will discover an inexhaustible source of strength. When you give yourself the permission to love who you are and what you look like without fear of judgment and rejection from mediocre men, that's when you begin to actually *live*, not just exist, and enjoy life.

We live in a world full of body shaming, and the severity and real-life implications of this particular form of discrimination can be seen everywhere. Fatphobia, for example, is ingrained in all kinds of different systems of oppression around the world. Our society is enormously fatphobic, from the way our health-care system cares (and doesn't care) for fat people to the endless cycles of diet trends and weight-loss programs marketed toward women and femmes. We are celebrated whenever we show up looking thinner, no matter what the drop in weight says about our actual health. It is, very sadly, a universal experience.

There's probably not a single person reading this book over the age of eighteen who has not at some point in their life seen their weight fluctuate and experienced the incredibly sad truth about how we're treated and rewarded socially when we lose weight, showing up to spaces we've previously occupied now smaller than we were before, whether it's intentional or not. No one cares if you were just training for a marathon or recently had a tapeworm infection. Same results, same comments. It's unanimous: *You look great!*

Women and femmes are forever praised for being perceived as thinner no matter the obvious and incredibly dangerous consequences. On the flip side, when we gain weight it's always flagged as reason for concern or as a sign that our health is in decline. The way fatphobia brainwashes even the most well-intentioned people into believing they're doctors after they see someone they know gain a lot of weight is shocking. No one gets a medical degree or nutritionist license faster than a fatphobic person who noticed you gained a lot of weight. And regardless of the reason for gaining weight, it should never be something society gets to use as a reason to treat you like shit. The inner workings of someone's physical health and mental health are not information strangers are entitled to, and they never will be in my space.

We all deserve so much better than this, and our weight should never come to define us. Bodies fluctuate, so you need to be rock solid in yourself. Never let this patriarchal world celebrate you for taking up less space.

Body neutrality is a practice, and an ongoing one at that. Too many of the conversations women/femmes have with one another about their bodies come from a place of sympathy or forced reassurance. How many times in our lives have we heard a bestie worry that they *look fat*? That their teeth, nose, thighs, whatever, are the true source of their problems in life, and what's holding them back from attaining the confidence they want and the partner they wish they had. Now more than ever, we need to be reminded that our bodies are not the enemy. They were not made to conform to or to fit into arbitrary parameters. Modern culture in the age of filters and Facetune—not unlike the age of thigh gaps and Victoria's Secret shows that came before it, or the age of glorified extreme thinness and liquid diets that came before that—wants us to be insecure so it can profit off of us. Following that path is not only fruitless, but also empty. At the end you'll see the true tea, which is: you will never be enough. So my advice is to abandon that path and forge a new one. One that is full of patience, love, and empathy. Because that is what you deserve.

Today, I try to believe my body is nothing more than a shell that holds all the most important parts of myself as a human. It's neither negative nor positive. Like it or not, it just is. And that is more than enough. The male gaze has historically been how many of us determine our own worth, causing us to spiral in our perceptions of our own bodies as well as the bodies of other women, even of those we don't know, like the famous women who we've been invited by our culture to objectify for eons. It's wild to me that we are literally responsible for bringing forth life onto this earth and yet are so consistently and relentlessly devalued for the parts of our bodies that aren't aesthetically ideal in the eyes of misogynistic men. It makes me mad, sure, but it also makes me realize that I need to be strong and steadfast in my practice.

Self-love and true confidence are not only the goals and destinations you want to come to, they're also ever-growing and -changing journeys. They twist and turn, and go up and down, but the final destination never wavers.

It's almost like when you're on a boat, and you're getting seasick, and they tell you to focus on the shoreline. The idea behind this is that it never moves, it's steady and permanent, and if you focus on that, you don't feel as nauseated. That's how I want to view my relationship with my body. Although the process can be arduous and upsetting at times, so much so it makes me sick, the shoreline keeps me sane. It reminds me over and over again that the goal shouldn't be to place my physical appearance in the highest regard. It's to know and believe that the physical form is impermanent and fickle.

I don't enjoy the fact that our bodies are the first things about ourselves that get judged on a daily basis, but at least I have the ability to lessen the importance I place on my own perception of my physical appearance. I would so much rather have my confidence rooted within than hope that a positive opinion about my own looks will be enough to carry me through life. Because everything about my inner self—my integrity, the love I have to give, my wit, my humor—those things are steady. They're consistent, and they matter far, far more.

8

IT'S OKAY TO BE MEAN

From a young age, we, as women, learn to prioritize other people ahead of ourselves, compromising our own boundaries out of fear of how we'll be perceived. In other words: most of us live in fear of being thought of as a "bitch." But the alternative is so much fucking worse. When we fail to learn to assert ourselves early and often, we run the risk of falling into patterns that expect us to cautiously tiptoe around boundary negotiations with others, terrible men especially, and this applies to straight-up lunkheads just as much as it does to insufferable "nice guys," both of whom I'll dissect in great detail in this chapter, as I ask the question: What is so wrong with being mean?

Now, if you know me from my persona online, you know that I'm a menace. I'm ruining dudes' days all the time, and people are still in shock that I'm mean. You wanna know who can't take a joke? Talk a walk on over to my page. All it takes is me telling men they look like they work at the movies and drive a Kia Soul and suddenly *I'm* the worst. But those who love me and my content get why I do it, and more specifically they get why I do it *that* way, while unfunny men with heads shaped like Abraham Lincoln's hat grow defensive and routinely call me a *fat bitch* who went *too far*. And when they respond with nothing more than fatphobia and vapid insults, because that's all their bird brains can think of, I laugh. I think to myself, *That's what you got? Why are you so upset? I thought we were all just making jokes and having a silly, goofy time. I thought we were double Dutching and this was my turn.* I tell them, *You and me? We could've been like Corbin Bleu and Keke Palmer in the Disney Channel Original Movie* Jump In! *Why'd you suddenly decide to take your ropes and go home? I thought we were having fun.*

These men are easily offended but completely ignore the fact that *their* jokes come at the expense of others and with real-life implications of racism, sexism, fatphobia, homophobia— you name it, they've tried it. I'm at a place in my life where I don't give a shit what men like this have to say about *anything*, and for that reason, my biggest complaint about being called *fat bitch*, aside from the fact that "fat" is not an insult, is simply that it isn't creative. It's just . . . so weak. Like their calves. That shit couldn't even get you onstage with a D-market all-male improv comedy troupe performing in front of a sausage-fest audience. I know for a fact that I am an incredible sparring partner, but the second I put these dudes on their toes, they have no jokes left. Why? Well, first, because I'm funny and they're not. And second, and most importantly, because what we do is fundamentally not the same.

When I make videos online defending fat people who were attacked—unprovoked—by awful men, of course I comment on their physical appearance. I give them a mere taste of their own judgment—often comparing them to cartoon characters and implying that they're ugly (because, to me, they are)—and whenever I do, these men emotionally crumble. They started it—you would think they'd laugh along with me, right? Wrong. Men's-rights-activist types especially love to get up in arms about this and accuse me of body shaming, but, babe, you can't call what I'm doing "body shaming" and what you did "jokes."

These men get mad—and violent—when I go after them. Countless men have sent me death threats, listing out all the ways they want to harm me, while continuously commenting on my weight as well. They use their perception of my body as grounds to inflict even greater harm on me because, at the end of the day, fatphobia isn't *just* mean jokes. It is a prevalent and violent system ingrained in all kinds of social, medical, and governmental systems all over. No one's body shaming you for having small feet or a tiny dick. When there's discrimination and suffering at the hands of systemic oppression, *then* it's no longer a joke.

Trying to equate the experience of body shaming that fat people endure every day to that of ugly men is like comparing getting run over to getting a flat tire. One is merely an inconvenience; the other could literally kill you. Are both not great? Sure. But we can all agree that one is infinitely worse than the other. Terrible men aren't oppressed by my taunting in the slightest; they're just insecure. They project those insecurities onto those farther down the oppression ladder because it makes them feel good. And where do insecure men love to hang out? On the internet.

Since the advent of social media, the internet has been a minefield for anyone who is not a cisgendered heterosexual white man. It can be a scary, dark, horrible place because even when we feel like we're safe in our own communities, there is always some asshole who sneaks past security and inserts himself into the conversation to say awful shit to marginalized people for no fucking reason. As someone who makes a living by fumigating the internet of these human roaches, I always say, I have the most aggressive form of job security there is because men will never stop being terrible, and I will never stop calling them out for it. I sleep soundly at night on a mattress that those bitches paid for.

Back in 2018, there was a quote being passed around that was attributed to Margaret Atwood, who at the time was witnessing her novel *The Handmaid's Tale* becoming one of the biggest shows on television. It went, "Men are afraid women will laugh at them. Women are afraid men will kill them." It was from an essay she had published over *forty years ago*. In true dystopian fashion, women around the world suddenly remembered what had never stopped being true. Women's greatest fear is violence or being murdered. But men's biggest fear? *Ridicule.* I don't know what further proof you need of the patriarchy having brainwashed us all. We're told from a young age that boys who tease girls do so out of romantic interest and that it's not uncommon to expect that will happen. As much of a nightmare scenario as this is, it's an unfortunate reality. They can dish it out, but they can't take it.

We have got to stop living in fear of being labeled as "mean" or "bitches," when it comes to prioritizing the feelings of men over ourselves. There are plenty of men who are self-aware enough to know how strong their point of privilege is, and who don't take advantage of all that they probably could get away with in our society. But the way terrible men treat women, and marginalized people especially, is a spell they have cast on all women and femmes that's put them to sleep. I am here to turn on the lights and wake all of you up—it's quite literally the job I get paid to do on the internet—but I want you all to know you also have this power. You just have to not only know where the switch is, but also be willing to turn it on. And it starts with you throwing out the notion that it's on *you* to protect men's masculinity by making yourself smaller. Don't dim your light so inferior men won't have to cover their eyes in your presence.

The truth is, terrible men are the way they are in part because they feel they have no agency in their own lives. They feel overlooked and mediocre, and so they cast aspersions on marginalized people because our resilience and joy are constant reminders to misogynists that they will never be exceptional. These men will never know true love, success, or happiness. The irony of their displaced anger is that their insults and words are just as mediocre as their lives, and that's why they hate people like us. Let's say you're a star athlete who plays every game for your team: Are you ever going to take advice from someone who's never seen the field? Someone who's never had a minute of playing time? Of course not! Never take criticism or advice from someone who isn't living the life you want. Their words are worthless, just like their insults. The longer you convince yourself that these men have feelings worth sparing, the longer you are going to be stuck in a constant cycle of disrespecting yourself.

My critics, primarily men, but sometimes women, too, love to list reasons why my approach "doesn't work." You see, there's this misunderstanding they've all come to believe that someone like myself—who has built a platform off of responding to hate directed at me personally as well as other marginalized people—is concerned about the well-being of antagonistic bigots. And that couldn't be further from the truth. I am not trying to fix these men. I don't care at all how terrible men operate in their daily lives. I am not invested in their mental growth, their hopes and dreams. Do I have big red frizzy hair and a fun, quirky outfit on? I don't, right? That's because I'm not Ms. Frizzle. I'm not their teacher. I'm not their mom. It is not my responsibility to educate them. I do this for other women, femmes, and everyone else who is *not* a bigot.

When any one of my many critics can list an example of a time when being nice to a bigot made them stop projecting their hateful views onto others, let me know. I can speak from experience that it has never worked for me, and I do not plan on continuing to test the waters to see if it does. You can talk all day to a terrible man, but you can't make him see you as a human. We can't make men respect us as people with agency and complex interiority when they only want to see us as objects. But we can embarrass them. And as someone who has built a literal career off of it, I can say with the utmost certainty now, this way is much more effective in the long run.

Let's take a look at what being a "mean-ass bitch" might look like for you when you encounter four different types of terrible men: The scary guy. The "nice guy" The guy who gives you an unforgivable ick. And the there's-no-saving-him guy.

The Scary Guy

This man approaches you in moments when you seem vulnerable, thus scaring the living shit out of you. He shows up when you are alone, or out at night by yourself, and always in a situation where it is not worth gambling on how a man might react. This can include moments like being catcalled on the street, approached in public when you're alone, etc. Y'all know the exact man I'm describing. As someone who has been afraid for my personal safety, as well as for those around me, in moments like this, I do have a solution. One that does not endanger you, but doesn't force you to speak to this man, either. It's called "pretend you can't hear him," and I've found it to be the most efficient way to deflect the scary guy's attempts at objectifying you. A simple "*What?*" repeated over and over again, after every "compliment" he tries to force you to engage with, is extremely efficient at wearing down the enemy without directly antagonizing him.

Many people can attest how being nice in moments like this, because you don't want to upset him, can sometimes have the opposite reaction or outcome from what we want. My approach avoids feeding his ego altogether and, most importantly, it protects you when you are in a vulnerable position.

When he throws unwanted attention your way, just pretend you can't hear him. The more confused you make him, the better. It creates a smoke screen for you to get out of there, and usually leaves him feeling stupid. This is psychological warfare that I can approve of. When men sense ridicule happening in subtle, quiet ways they can't grasp, it not only haunts them, but distracts them long enough that you can leave quickly. I always advise my baddies to implement tactics like this for safety reasons, but please know and understand that men can be unpredictable and dangerous. Always prioritize your safety over their feelings!

The "Nice Guy"

Being nice and being kind are two different things. The former often has to do with perception, whereas the latter more often than not stems from a person's actions. I have always found being kind is much more important, because anyone can be "nice." It's easily faked and seemingly nice people don't always have good intentions.

A prime example of this is the "nice guy." For him, being nice is what I *actually* consider to be the bare minimum. When self-proclaimed nice guys try to tout how well they treat women especially, they're just bragging about basic human decency in my eyes. Oh, you didn't interrupt her when she was telling you about her day? You didn't mention that you think she's gained weight? You didn't comment on how much you didn't like the sandwich she made for you? Give me a fucking break. No one is handing out gold medals for that.

This man is polite and overly nice, essentially just in the

beginning, in an attempt to get you to think that how he's acting is the very best behavior you'll ever get out of a man, even if it's just common manners and tact. He has the audacity to say things like *Well, I was so nice to her, I cleaned up after myself and never said how boring her stories were and she still left . . . I guess women just don't want a "nice guy" these days.* Do you see the manipulation embedded in that sentence? This man is describing basic human decency, but it's being weaponized as a reason women should settle. Fuck that. You deserve treatment, love, and care that are equal to what you give. You are *worthy* of that, and should settle for nothing less!

Words are not the same as actions, and "nice guys" are almost never genuinely good men. Their act is so thin and transparent that if you've ever dealt with one of them, you can learn to spot the rest of them the second they open their mouths, if not sooner. From the way they look to the way they talk to the way they breathe, they may be telling you they're nice, but talk is cheap. And would you believe how many of these guys actually believe their inherent "niceness" is what is keeping them from landing the girl of their dreams?

Let's be clear: a "nice guy" is just as capable of objectifying women as an unapologetic douchebag. For any readers who may not have encountered this type of horrible man out there in the real world yet, let me tell you what millions of us have already realized to be true about this particular dude: he won't stop if you're not interested. This type of terrible man believes in his heart of hearts that it's within his power to get you to change your mind. That you don't know what you really want, but *he does.* If you don't like him, for whatever reason, he intends to make you feel guilty to the point of acquiescence. He will try to convince you that your swift, rather than polite and overly nice, rejection is rude and dismissive. How dare you not even give him a chance!

But your succumbing to this coercion is his goal. Do not cave. Not everyone can handle confrontation like me, and I am more than aware of that. So it isn't realistic to expect all of you to tell men like this to suck your wiener and fuck off (although I wish it could be). My goal is never to change you and turn you into me; it's to equip you with the knowledge and understanding that you deserve all the love and respect you want. This includes not allowing men to talk you into compromising your own boundaries.

Any sugarcoating done in the service of a man like this only enables him and convinces him that you've left the door slightly open to have your mind changed. No one outside of your own person should be talking about what it is *you* want. Pretending to be nice to a man who you are in fact rejecting emboldens him in his quest to violate your boundaries. As hard as it may be to stand firm in your rejection, remind yourself that your comfort matters. You don't owe him an explanation, excuse, or reason. The word "no" is a complete sentence.

The Guy Who Gives You an Unforgivable Ick

These men, as their name implies, are the ones who, if not instantly then suddenly all at once, fill you with unpleasantness. They give you *the ick*. Sort of like emotional food poisoning, only there's no bouncing back after forty-eight hours. The thing about the ick is that it's usually triggered by seemingly superficial behaviors, and not from discovering the explicit flaws in someone's core value systems. Like if I find out a man's a bigot? I don't have the ick, I just hate him. You might not always understand the logic behind the ick, but I have reason to believe this is your body's evolutionary response to being put off by men in your dating pool. It mustn't be ignored. You need to learn to obey (or at least pay attention to) it—even if trying to describe it makes you feel nuts.

For example, I once stopped speaking to a guy after hearing him make up a word midconversation with me. We had been talking for weeks and decided to hang out after class and he was right in the middle of telling me how smart he was when he dropped the bomb on me. I can't remember exactly what he said, because, again, it was NOT A REAL WORD, but visceral disgust coursed through my veins. I was so repulsed by the audacity of this guy to talk down to me as if my small woman brain would never be able to compute his otherworldly intelligence, while simultaneously making up words like a caveman. How incredibly condescending he was, assuming I wouldn't pick up on something as silly as a made-up word.

Men get so irrationally angry when women and femmes describe the ick, and accuse us of being picky or unreasonable, and that they shouldn't be judged on one momentary lapse. And it's true, the guy who made up a word midconversation with me probably isn't a *bad* person, just as the guy at the gym who assumed my personal trainer friend couldn't possibly lift the weights she was working with or the guy on the first date who can't stop talking about how many dates he's been on but he's still single isn't, either. But it's not about how women and femmes should continue giving men chances just because they've cleared the lowest possible bar of humanity. It's about letting that seemingly irrational ick help you say no.

When you catch the ick, you may feel compelled to deliberate and run through a bunch of different scenarios in your head to try to talk yourself out of the fact that you were just majorly turned off. I think an issue we run into a lot is people implying that this kind of veto system is void of patience. Some people truly do need to be given a chance in order to truly be seen for who they are, and that I am all for. The problem I have with this kind of leniency, though, is that it leaves no room for women and femmes to act on red flags without fear of criticism. The ick is primal, and there's no moving past it. You have every right to kick his ass to the curb if you so choose.

The There's-No-Saving-Him Guy

This man needs no introduction and there's simply no way around it: he fully sucks. Here in the US, we have our assorted alpha males, gym bros, and hypermasculine podcast host types, but the earth is full of men like this and their variety is seemingly endless. What they all have in common is the disease of internalized (and heavily externalized) misogyny.

He is desperate to cling to power and hopelessly reliant on the approval of other men he idealizes. He sees you as a plaything and nothing more. Women exist as accessories, and whether or not we have thoughts, feelings, or ambitions is of no concern to him. You should be able to pick this man out of a lineup easily, so I'm not too concerned about that. What I am concerned about here, though, is whether or not he will still feel entitled to something from you.

Every confident woman in this world has taken *hundreds* of necessary steps to unlearn what society initially told her was correct. From not taking up too much space, to only feeling validated by male approval—no matter what her background is, I guarantee she has worked to overcome patriarchal bullshit by digging deep within herself and defining what it means to be a woman/femme, free of male validation. This confidence does not come at the expense of anyone else's; it does not dim or stomp out other people's lights. It shines strongly and proudly, all on its own. However, terrible men are enraged by this mindset. They don't know how to harness strength or power unless it involves ripping it out of someone else. Because they have no self-worth outside of punching down, they are never satisfied unless they feel better than someone else, and a lot of times that means women.

If you're anything like me, you probably feel nothing but blind rage toward this man because he's the biggest proponent of this fucked-up patriarchal system we live within. He is so far up his own ass, he can't see how he's been held back in every aspect of his life. He will refuse to acknowledge how the patriarchy, although it's a system built and upheld by his peers, has negative effects on him as well. The patriarchy does not discriminate when it comes to who it hurts, but it does have one target it intentionally is trying to harm. These men hold the same ideologies as ones who are pro-military but don't have anything to say about mental health advocacy or the homelessness crisis for veterans. The same men who weep when they hear short guy jokes but laugh hysterically at fat-phobic ones. The same men only care about bullying when it comes to me attacking bigots but feel zero remorse for those who get bullied for just existing as someone outside of the very shallow parameters of cis, thin, and white.

I do not, and will not ever, feel bad for this man. And neither should you. He's hurt enough people in life up until this point, and his hardwiring is faulty. It's not our job, or our responsibility, to learn how to rewire him. All that ends up happening in that case is we get electrocuted. What I choose to do instead is recognize that this man is a grown adult, with a fully functioning brain, who makes his own choices, and those choices happen to include being a bigot. So as a fellow grown adult, with a fully functioning brain, I choose to humiliate the shit out of him for upholding these violent systems of oppression. I highly encourage you all to do the same. Because even though some men, or even women, will enable and encourage this kind of behavior, I refuse to. Staying silent in the face of active and sinister oppression is not something I'll be taking to my grave. Will you?

Terrible men only see you if they feel like they can use you for something, whether that's physical or emotional, and even then, they don't see you as a sentient human. They see you as a tool. The moment they let on to this fact, and you recognize this red-flag behavior, you need to cauterize the end of your respect for them. Burn it immediately. If terrible men are going to disrespect your boundaries regardless, you might as well come out swinging. Don't soften it. Men like this expect you to consistently make them feel comfortable and prioritize their feelings, and why should you have to? Stop being afraid. When people ask me if I'm ever bothered by being perceived as mean, I always answer the same way: I *am* mean. I have all the capability in the world to be mean, just like everyone else. What I think matters most, and what is a true measure of integrity, is how we choose to use it. So yes, I am very fucking mean, especially to terrible men, and they would do well to remember that.

Saying what you really think and feel does you a lot more good than being forced to act sweet when it's actually just passive. We're often told that sticking to the latter makes us the "bigger person." But why should the person being disrespected have to remain accommodating and patient, regardless of how men make us feel? (That's a rhetorical question, by the way—we both know the answer to this.) Instead, I want you to be a different kind of bigger person, a more literal one. Like when you see a bear in the woods, the advice is to get big—push back your shoulders, raise your arms above your head, and yell loudly. A similar approach works when you encounter terrible men—you gotta get big to get them to back down. Stand tall, clear your head, and let them have it. You don't need to feel guilty about not mincing words. Remember, if you were a guy, people would call you fearless and hilarious. Women deserve the freedom to speak bluntly and directly, especially when they're being openly disrespected. Being mean is an effective tool for asserting the dominance that exists within all of us, but especially when it comes to protecting and standing up for ourselves. We are so much stronger and more capable than the patriarchy would have us believe.

It's not a new phenomenon for confident women who don't allow themselves to be walked all over to be referred to as "mean." If you know in your heart that you are kind, you never need to waste your time trying to act palatable or gain the favor of men by always being "nice." When I was growing up, my mom was incredibly vocal and hell-bent on advocating for anyone she saw being mistreated or harmed out in public. I only have memories of my dad hanging back without saying a word, and I took note: men who are secure within themselves and who don't draw power from pushing down their female partners aren't intimidated when women speak up. He never felt threatened by my mom's ability to assert herself, and he would never even think to criticize that behavior like a lot of men do when they see women calling out shit that they don't like. My boyfriend is of the same mindset. I wouldn't have it any other way. If y'all are with a guy who has a problem with you advocating for yourself or for others in times when you witness disrespect or rudeness occurring right in front of you, that's a red flag. If they ever make you feel *crazy* or call you inappropriate for sticking up for what's right, even if it's in public—run! Ask yourself: Why does this man feel *embarrassed* when his partner is standing up for herself and for others? You're not spewing entitlement or expecting more than you're owed. You're standing up for those that can't stand up for themselves, and there is no shame in that heroic action. So if he's not on your side, well, whose side is he on exactly?

Anyway, back to my mom, the first woman who showed me the power of wielding hostility to get what's fair, sorted, and in order. Our family didn't have a lot of money when I was younger, and in elementary school Deison and I received free and reduced-price lunch. But there was a problem. Several days in a row, my sister came home starving. Our mom was confused and kept asking why Deison hadn't eaten more at school. Eventually, she let it slip that there was a girl asking for her lunch who would tell Deison that if she didn't give it to her, she wouldn't be her friend. Fearing she'd already said too much, Deison declined to elaborate further, so my mom recruited me for a special mission: find out who was taking her lunch. And of course *I was on it.*

At school the next day I went to sit with my sister's class, a full grade older than my own. Lo and behold, a girl walks up and tells Deison she wants her lunch. Stepping in as my sister's own personal bodyguard, I tell her, "No, Deison's not giving you her lunch today. And by the way, no one wants to be your friend anyway." Then, to really finish her off, I called her "Stuart Little." She was small, compared to me, at least, the biggest kid in the goddamn school. But really it was just the first mean thing that came to mind. She immediately burst into tears and ran over to a nearby teacher to report my crimes. I got in trouble, but that didn't really matter. My mom was there to bail me out. When I reported back and gave her the full rundown after school that day, she did her best to not laugh at my "Stuart Little" quip. She did tell me I shouldn't call people names, but I could tell she was proud. The job was done. Little did I know at the time that sticking up for my sister against other kids our age who wanted to take advantage of her kindness would be the training ground for my inevitable future of standing up for others and bullying the bullies. Even then, I think deep down I knew that there was power in empowering others, an example that was always set by my amazing mom.

I swear to you, I never saw this woman take shit from *anyone*. She was brave, bold, and unapologetically herself. In middle school, there was a period of time when I was being flagged for dress code violations nearly every other day. Over the summer, I'd hit a growth spurt, and now all my hemlines fell just short of what was considered "appropriate" on a pre-teen girl. When the school finally called my mom into the front office to address this, she was having *none of it*. She wasted zero energy making nice with the administrators and came right out and told them, "You are targeting my daughter." Were the smaller, shorter girls who wore the same hemlines getting written up? Not at all, because the policing of our bodies starts very early, especially for those of us who develop earlier than others. My clothing fell just short because of how much I'd grown, and even then was still not inappropriate by any means. I was just a lot easier to spot. My mom fought for me. She told the school they were using an archaic ideal of dressing that wasn't appropriate for adolescent girls whose clothes will naturally ride up and shrink against their growing frames. And she was not about to go out and buy me all-new clothes over this. She shut it down. My shorts weren't deterring anyone from accomplishing what they needed to at school. And if they were that big of a distraction? Well, then the problem lay elsewhere, didn't it?

My mom's gone to bat for me like this more times in my life than I can count, and she does this for family, friends, and strangers alike. She's absolutely fearless in the face of injustice, and always willing to put her neck on the line to stand up for what's right. Never once has she been afraid of what other people think or her own reputation, and she's remained candid with my sister and me ever since we were little about how we should never measure the opinions of others against how we, most importantly, see ourselves in this world. Because only one person's opinion matters: yours.

I tell these stories now not to convince you that I come from a long line of mean old bitches, but to demonstrate how it's possible to rewrite the norms and define for yourself how you react in the face of discrimination and disrespect, whether that's coming from terrible men, maladapted women living under the patriarchy, or anyone else who decides to bully others for no reason. What I want for you all to understand is that being kind and patient with men who are openly disrespectful to you or anyone else, unwarranted, is an entitlement, not a requirement. It is a consequence of the many oppressive systems that have been ingrained in our society for those who sit higher on the ladder to feel power when they punch down. This emotional warfare is not our responsibility to take on. These kinds of men don't deserve the patience or kindness they're requiring of you, when they can't offer it themselves. And despite all of the love, support, and sterling examples I grew up with, nothing could have prepared me, when I left home, for just how truly vile men could be out in the wild, even in the workplace.

I had a lot of different menial jobs throughout school and right after college. I went door-to-door for a PR firm (where I also worked with my sister and for my mom), alerting residents to upcoming freeway construction in their area. I dressed up as Disney's Moana for children's birthday parties, performing to the max of my abilities without actually having to sing any songs from the film (because I can't sing for shit). I worked eight-to-ten-hour shifts as a food server, after which I would ride the bus home at 11:00 p.m., exhausted but hypervigilant as I contemplated the potential horrors of traveling alone at night as a woman. But nowhere left me feeling as exposed to casual misogyny as my time in sports media. As soon as I started working in *that* industry, I began hearing the most condescending things said in the workplace by grown men who truly believed they were delivering compliments. A new male coworker actually said to me, "Hey, you know, you're a lot smarter than you look. I don't see that a lot in women who look like you. It's impressive." This was, mind you, said to me as I was training him on how to do *my* job. He was new to my team, and he needed help. And yet, he somehow assumed the default dynamic between us would be him bestowing backhanded respect upon me, for which I would likely feel flattered and charmed. The irony is so violent it makes my teeth hurt. Immediately, I clapped back, "Was that supposed to be a compliment? Because it wasn't." He picked the wrong woman to try to alienate from her pack. I am 100 percent always with and for the girls. You know how pick-mes say things like *I'm so not like other girls, I'm more of a guys' girl*? I'm the opposite of that. I am *just* like every other bitch you know. In fact, I'm worse.

This ended up being one of my first experiences being up front and blunt, or *mean*, as the terrible men like to frame it, in the workplace, and I truly believe it is a mindset women and femmes have to master the minute we enter the job market to guard and protect our overall well-being. When I initially shared this story, plenty of people I knew told me that they thought I had overreacted and should have just kept the peace. What if I had lost my job? What if he got offended and told my supervisor he no longer wanted to work there because I had created a hostile work environment? Was my response worth losing my income? To all of that, the answer seemed simple: Who cares? Who cares if I lost my job because of that? Did I want to work in a place that would unabashedly support men harassing their coworkers like that? (Obviously, this is a mindset that is easy to hold when you're young and have fewer responsibilities financially, but the principle is what is important.) The reality of this situation was extremely simple to me: I was being sexually harassed and disrespected, so I was going to respond, quickly and rudely. That's it. I've never been okay with disrespect, but I'm especially not okay with it in the workplace coming from men. In the words of the great artist Kelis: "You don't have to love me . . . [or] like me . . . but you will respect me."

Here's the thing. In certain situations, work being a key example, it usually benefits everyone to communicate and give feedback to one another in a manner that is kind and never overly harsh, because, all else being equal, colleagues want to establish mutual respect and a nice rapport with one another. The last thing anyone ever wants is a hostile work environment, which is never lost on me. You would do the same for a friend, keeping their feelings in mind when you deliver criticism or broach a difficult subject. As you would for a partner, who you are building a relationship with and probably navigating different communication styles alongside. This is exactly why behavior that is rude, harmful, and backhanded—in a single word, *unprofessional*—must be called out immediately in the workplace. There is a code to be honored in interpersonal relationships of any kind, and as far as I'm concerned, once that's broken, all bets are off. You cannot be expected to just internalize the harmful shit that someone else started, let alone continue to work alongside them as if nothing happened.

Now, I know you may be thinking, *Well, Drew, that's not being mean exactly. I thought this chapter was about coming out swinging!* As much as I'm delighted by the thought that my content makes it look easy, being mean in an effective manner requires tons of thought and preparation. You must study the enemy.

And, look, I get it: strategically calculating just how mean you get to be in any given environment may initially seem like just as much work as being palatable and nice. But the truth of the matter is that it's work simply to exist as a woman or femme in this world. Labor, both physical and emotional, is hidden in everything we do, but so much of it is defaulted in the service of men. And that's why this chapter as well as this entire book are so important to me—I've put it into the world as your emotional support guide to help you in your journey toward decentering men. Just think about all the moments you've spent reeling in pent-up emotions—like anger, angst, and internalized aggression—after realizing how much of your behavior that day was spent accommodating men. Like my therapist always reminds me, "When your needs are consistently not being met, you end up turning into the person you most fear you may actually be."

Getting to be mean in whatever capacity you most effectively can is a great way to let a lot of that internal rage out. I always compare myself to a venomous snake: in order to be the best version of myself for the world, I must expel my venom. Never feel bad for standing up for yourself or for standing up for others, because it's never in vain, even if it can feel like it at the time. You are worth the respect that you so freely give to others, so if someone refuses to give that to you as a fellow human, then offer it to yourself in the form of advocacy. I hope that people continue to come my way for the courage to truly allow themselves this freedom. I'll always be here to remind you: Being mean is not always required, but sometimes it's necessary. And there's nothing wrong with that!

9

THERE'S NO ONE WAY TO BE A WOMAN BUT ONLY ONE WAY TO BE YOURSELF

There have been times I've been accused of putting on an act or playing up certain parts of myself. But I actually think the reason I've found the community I have is *because* I am 100 percent myself. I won't work with brands who don't understand that, and believe me, I've missed out on opportunities for being too loud and controversial. But I'd rather never make a cent from social media again than compromise who I am or what I believe in, and/or put the people I love in harm's way.

That being said, there are some parts of my life that I am hesitant to reveal widely. For anything I share about my family and Pili, I always make sure to have their consent. I would hate for the career I've chosen or the choices I've made to impact them in any kind of negative way, especially if that were to happen without their consent. It's why I rarely talk about or even show certain people in or around my family, because while I may have signed up for this career and life-style, they did not. Even though they all have front-row seats to what I go through on the daily, it's still my responsibility to do everything I can to draw proper boundaries and protect the people I love.

The same goes for myself. Everything I share is completely authentic, but that doesn't mean I share everything. Especially as a woman, every one of my choices, opinions, and statements can and will be scrutinized, judged, and attacked far more than they would be for any male counterpart. And especially as a plus-size woman of color, I am extra vulnerable to misogyny that is compounded with racism and fatphobia.

Even though I'm proud of the work I've done in divesting myself from the patriarchy, I will freely admit that I have beliefs that I have been hesitant to be fully honest about online because I am afraid of potential backlash. It hasn't been until recently that I've realized how important it is that I use my platform and speak up, especially about beliefs that I know for sure I am not the only one to hold but that some women may be hesitant to share because of the possible response from terrible men. But I want them to know that they are not alone in these thoughts, and their feelings are valid and real.

Truth be told, I don't want to be a mom. And I don't think I ever have.

Just writing that is so daunting, even now, as a woman in her late twenties who has known this about herself for a long time. There is an unspoken, undeniable taboo that's attached to thoughts like that, especially as a woman living in a patriarchal world.

When women talk about not wanting children for any reason, the world shames them. And this is something I've observed from people all across the political, religious, and cultural spectrums. Our society prioritizes bringing life into the world above all else, and doesn't accept that some people may choose not to have children simply because they don't want to. Which is a perfectly valid reason. Tell me if this sounds familiar, because I've heard it all: *You'll change your mind when you get older. There's no love in this world like being a mom. The minute you hold your newborn baby, it'll click. You just haven't met the right person yet. Don't wait too long, because then you'll regret it and it'll be too late.*

All of which I fully believe is true . . . for some people. I'm just not one of them. For a long time, I was actually convinced that the desire would come for me eventually, but years would pass, I would reach certain milestones, and still . . . nothing. I once felt anxiety about that because I had internalized all these things the world around me had told me about my worth and identity as a woman, let alone as a potential mother. But now I know that the same way that it doesn't matter how you dress, who you love, or how you choose to live your life as long as it doesn't actively hurt any other living being, it's okay not to want children.

It's not because I hate children or had a traumatic relationship with my parents, which seem to be the only two incredibly unimaginative reasons misogynistic people can come up with for why a young woman may not want to procreate. First of all, one of the reasons I am so grateful for my platform is because it allows me to reach and impact young people in particular, and second of all, you know by now how amazing my parents were. But, put simply, I believe in a woman's right to choose. That's it. Anyone who doesn't want to have children should have their desire respected instead of questioned.

The "ticking clock" metaphor is one that I bristle at. It assumes that all women aspire to motherhood, while limiting the role to those with a uterus, and reducing the value that women have to their ability to conceive. Plus, many women simply don't want children, and it's a mentality that I wish people would stop treating like a villainous and selfish act. We should not feel forced to adhere to a child-rearing life simply because that's what all women are expected to want. And while it is true that age is a factor in one's ability to get pregnant and give birth, everyone acts as if you become infertile once you hit your thirties, when how and if your age might affect your pregnancy is fully a conversation between no one but you, your doctor, and your partner if having children is a dream you have. Plus, there are any number of options available nowadays, including IVF, egg freezing, and surrogacy (though obviously many of these options are gate-kept by money and access). I'm not saying that the push to have children young is deliberate misinformation, but there are many damaging beliefs that surround that desire, like wanting to "bounce back from your pregnancy body" or be a "young and hot" mom.

Also, this obsession with biological childbirth erases so many other forms of parenthood and family. I know so many people who have fulfilling relationships as stepparents, adoptive parents, or aunts/uncles. I also know of families that have two moms, two dads, nonbinary parents, or single parents as well. The outdated idea of a heterosexual nuclear family as the only way to raise children is yet another by-product of colonization, white supremacy, and misogyny. While I may not have any plans to have children of my own, I am so excited to be an auntie to any children my sister or my brother or best friends may choose to have. It turns out that when you stop believing the lie that women are on some kind of strict timeline, the world opens up to you and what it is you *really* want.

When I look back at my childhood, I remember many instances when I wanted to be the mom, whether that was when we played house or when I proudly called myself the mom of my friend group. I used to equate that to a natural proclivity toward being a parent. Now, looking at it through a clearer lens, I realize that it wasn't being a mom I was striving toward. It was being in charge and the leader. I wanted to be the decision-maker in my life, and I equated that with being a mom.

And this makes sense, because as y'all know by now, *my* mom has always been the boss, a bad bitch, and a woman whose capacity for generosity has inspired me my entire life. So, because that was the example I had growing up, to me, that's what a mom was: the most confident, assured person in the room. A mom was someone who, above all else, stood up for others. Those traits were ones I have tried to emulate for as long as I can remember. I don't think my adolescent brain really understood the difference between wanting to be *my* mom and wanting to be *a* mom. It was as I grew older that I had to wrestle with the realization that wanting the former did not necessarily lead to the latter.

Going through high school and eventually college, I would constantly hear my friends say things like *I can't wait to be a mom.* They'd all sit around and share baby names or coo over baby clothes, none of which had ever crossed my mind to care about. All of this is very normal in theory, but to me it seemed so frivolous. Not because I think striving toward parenthood is superficial, but because I couldn't relate. Not even a little. I had never thought about what I would want my kids to be named, what I would want them to do with their lives, nothing. When I tried to even imagine what my child would look like, I would recoil . . . because I simply couldn't see it.

I remember actively thinking at one point that I had to make up answers to these questions, because it embarrassed me to not have any. Why was I the only person who never had these thoughts? Why was I seemingly the only person in my friend group who never brainstormed what my future kids would look like? Why did I actively dread the thought of childbirth and parenting? Was there something wrong with me? Even as I got older, I still chalked it up to me being young or a late bloomer in this respect. I was sure that one day, I would have all the answers. In my naivete, I was certain that when the time came, I would be ready. I would know.

But more time kept passing, and I entered into full adulthood still waiting for the moment when the desire for motherhood would arrive for me and I'd finally feel something when

I saw babies on the street. But it never came, not even a whisper of it, and I started to really question and think about why those thoughts were never something that came naturally in the first place and why I still thought it mattered so much. Why did it make me anxious to join in on my friends' conversations about their futures, which I knew would inevitably turn toward children and building a family? Why did it frustrate me to have these conversations at all even when I knew it made sense? After all, we were having these conversations in the context of long-term relationships, five-year plans, and what the future would hold. As a Virgo who loves planning ahead, shouldn't this have been right up my alley?

Now, looking back, I think part of my frustration was because it felt like motherhood was always talked of as the final destination. That it was where all women *should* end up, regardless of their initial dreams or ambitions. You could spend as much time in school as you wanted, you could work your ass off and climb the ladder professionally and be the most successful person in the room . . . but none of that would be worth anything if you didn't also have children. And this was a tricky expectation, one that even came from other women, for whom it seemed to be a particular point of pride to be able to balance a loving relationship, a successful career, and motherhood. The implication was that modern womanhood wasn't complete without all three. If you weren't a mother, what was it all even for? What was the point of living if you weren't living for others? Was the life that you built and worked so hard for worth anything if the final goal wasn't to be a mom?

That was my biggest struggle, because I just couldn't get

behind that ideology. I am a true supporter of any lifestyle that women want to lead: CEO, stay-at-home mom, both, neither, or something completely different. Whatever women want to pursue, as long as it doesn't harm anyone and isn't bigoted in any way, I support them. If that dream is motherhood, I sincerely support and admire that choice. But I am surprised to find that anytime I even suggest that my dream future does not involve parenting of any kind, I have been met with concern at best and disdain at worst. To think that the world wants me to believe that my true value and worth begin and end with what comes out of my uterus is asinine. It feels reductive and offensive to water down my dreams in order to fulfill an archaic idea of what it means to be a woman in this world.

What I am most surprised by is how often I receive this pushback from other women, whether they are fellow feminists or women I have nothing in common with. I am as loudly pro-choice as anyone can be, but even in those spaces, I have found that the conversation centers more on a woman's choice of *when* to have children, not on a woman's choice to have children at all.

And the argument from the other side is even worse—not only do people who hold antiabortion views seem to think that an unborn fetus's right to life is more important than the person carrying it, but the implication is that a woman who doesn't fulfill her alleged biological "duty" to have children is inhumane. It's incredibly damaging to treat the question of having children as a foregone conclusion, when instead we should be giving people the freedom to decide if having children makes sense emotionally, financially, and in every other way. After all, it's also not fair to the children themselves, who deserve to be born to parents who truly want them.

Parenthood is also connected to romantic companionship in a way that I find so limiting. For example, before I was able to articulate my thoughts on motherhood, I believed that as I started to date and eventually fell in love with Pili, the answers would come to me. At the time, I was still living under the impression that motherhood was my only option as a woman. So once Pili and I were together, I thought, *Now that I've found my soulmate, any day now I will be okay with having children.* Because everything I had consumed in my twenty-plus years of being alive at that point had told me that finding the right person would 100 percent catapult that thinking. I would finally be able to see myself becoming a mom, because my other half was now in my life, and what was even the point of dating and getting married if it wasn't going to end with building a family? The patriarchy even takes it a step further, and says that a woman who can't—or doesn't want to—give a man the family he wants shouldn't be surprised when he leaves her for someone who can.

I also want to acknowledge that while men are obviously given many more options for what their lives can look like, fatherhood is often pushed onto them as well. After all, a major part of the fantasy of masculinity involves being the head and breadwinner of a household that includes children who you can pass your wisdom and legacy on to without any sense for what a shared and equitable parenting style actually looks like. Putting aside the fact that there are lots of men who genuinely shouldn't be fathers at all, these expectations place pressure on men without first giving them the tools to succeed. It's another example of how specific patriarchal expectations limit how we *all* approach the world, not just women.

Because Pili and I knew very quickly that we wanted to be together no matter what, we knew we needed to discuss our stances on so many of the questions that affected not only our own individual futures, but also the one we wanted to build together. Because I'm me, and because Pili is Pili, committing to total transparency and shared responsibility in our relationship has always been our top priority. So from the beginning, we would have these essential, and sometimes terrifying, talks about the future. What did we see for ourselves? Did we fit into each other's ideas of the future? If so, were we willing to support each other in achieving those shared and individual goals?

Getting married was the first major question that came up for us, and our answers were exactly the same: absolutely. Pili told me that before us, he had never wanted to get married. And after our third date, he knew he was going to marry me. The sentiment was exactly the same on my end. With zero hesitation, I knew I wanted to spend the rest of my life with him. That decision felt like breathing: natural and necessary. Now, when it came to having children, it felt like the breathing hitched on both ends. Both of us weighed in as a big maybe. We were tentative. Always careful to consider the other person's feelings and leave the possibility open because we were both scared of fully closing the door if that wasn't what the other person wanted. We would always say things like, *I could see that happening.* Or, *If I was going to do that, I wouldn't want it to be with anyone but you.*

Still, the tenor of our conversations was never one of certainty. It was always a maybe. And what I know now is that if it isn't a fuck yes, it's a no. There's no waffling about bringing life into the world—you either want to or you don't. It's the very least you owe to yourself, because once you become a parent, you can't opt out, and your future child deserves to be brought into a world where they are wholeheartedly wanted and loved.

At that early point in our relationship, I still believed that it was possible to exist in this in-between space of uncertainty, because I wasn't yet in a place to fully own and be self-confident in my convictions. Unfortunately, I was forced to realize the necessity of enthusiastic consent when it comes to motherhood because of an experience I genuinely never thought I would have to go through.

One month, several years into dating Pili, my period was late. As a lifelong athlete, I was used to this, and it wasn't uncommon for my cycle to skip entire months altogether. But when you're in a long-term relationship, having an irregular period can be concerning for one very specific reason.

At first, I wasn't worried. This wasn't the first time this had happened, and in the past it always eventually came. But when days started to become weeks, and there was still no sign of my period, I began to grow anxious. To be safe, Pili bought me a pregnancy test. I still wasn't fully convinced, so even when I took it, I was trying my absolute best to not stress and told myself that it was all just a precaution.

But when it came time to check the results, I found that I couldn't look. So I asked Pili to . . . and his face turned white. The test was positive. When he told me, I legitimately thought he was kidding, but the look on his face was dead serious: my life was about to change. I didn't know what to say. He started pacing around the room as I just sat there in complete disbelief.

Finally, I broke the silence. The first words out of my mouth were "What're we going to do?" At that point, I think my question snapped him out of his stupor, because he came over and sat down next to me, held my hands, and said, "Whatever you want. Whatever you want to do, I'm here. I'll always be here, no matter what."

I completely broke down and just started sobbing as we held each other. Fear aside, I knew why I was crying, and so did he. I knew what I wanted. I didn't have the courage to say it out loud, but I knew without either of us verbalizing it.

As someone who is avidly pro-choice, I'm here to tell you and anyone who would ever think otherwise: choosing to have an abortion is not easy. It is not a decision you make lightly, and it's not one that feels good. It's one that, regardless of where you stand morally, can easily haunt you. Beyond the very real physical and medical consequences and possible complications, it is never fun emotionally or mentally to make a decision about something that will radically change your life. Getting an abortion means arriving at a fork in the road and needing to choose a path to go down, knowing that you can never go back. It's why I'm so frustrated by antiabortion stances that paint people who seek abortions as wishy-washy or weak. They treat it as if the level of physical, emotional, and mental anguish that goes into making a decision of that magnitude is easy to bear.

Pili understood that, and I remain so grateful that his first instinct was to reassure me that he would support whatever decision *I* made. As partners, this pregnancy would affect both our futures. But because I was the person in the relationship with the uterus, ultimately the decision was wholly mine to make, and he honored that. Pili's respect for my bodily autonomy in that moment reassured me that in our relationship, we were truly equal.

As I sat with this knowledge, there was a part of me that waited for even an ounce of excitement to bubble up through the apprehension. After all, wasn't this the moment that everyone who had ever said, *You'll feel differently when the time comes* was referring to? Well, the time had come. There was the possibility that I could have a child with the love of my life. And I felt nothing but dread and the fear that this experience had already changed my relationship and might change it even more drastically as a result of the choice I knew I had to make.

In all the times I had imagined what a successful, happy, and vibrant life for myself could look like, motherhood had always been conspicuously missing. So yes, I did have a breakthrough moment, but not the one I had been led to believe I'd have. I *did* realize that pursuing motherhood is so precious, so important, and so life-changing . . . and that's exactly why it isn't for me.

That was when I decided that having an abortion was

going to be the best course of action. I looked up the nearest women's health center, and they luckily had an appointment that day. Off we went. The drive there felt a million hours long, and we were both so shaken that we didn't even listen to music the entire time. Pili just held my hand and silently soothed me while I quietly cried the entire way there. When we pulled up, I had to go in alone. He assured me he would wait for me in the car, and be there for me no matter what I decided.

I went inside and met with the nurses, who were so kind and patient with me as I cried through my story. They let me know that the odds of having a false positive from a pregnancy test were slim to none, but still they would test me again just to be sure. The waiting process couldn't have taken longer than ten minutes at most, but it was excruciating. I kept wanting to get up from the chair, walk out of the health center, get back in the car with Pili, and ask him to drive us back to our lives and pretend none of this was happening, but that wasn't a choice, because it wasn't reality.

When the doctor came back with my results, she told me that my urine sample had come back negative. It had been a false positive. I wasn't pregnant after all.

I was out of my mind with relief, and if there was ever a moment that confirmed everything I had ever known about myself and my stance on being a mother, the overwhelming joy and relief I felt upon hearing I was not pregnant was it. I started crying in front of her, and she held my hand and told me everything was going to be okay, something so small and simple that truly meant a lot to me. The entire experience of sitting in that women's health center is one that I am grateful to have had, looking back now, solely because it was confirmation to me that women are so essential to this world. The care, patience, empathy, and support I felt on that afternoon, from women who didn't even know me but immediately recognized the situation I was in and were able to give me what I needed emotionally—I will be eternally grateful to those women. The emotional labor that women perform for others and the deep empathy they hold for literal strangers are things that touch me deeply. On that day, I needed them and they were there. I don't even know if they remember me, as I'm sure they see hundreds of women in situations like mine, but if any of you ladies ever read this book, please know how grateful I am. You have no idea how much you all did for me. From the bottom of my heart, thank you.

That day was a pivotal moment for me, and not just because it gave me final clarity on how I felt about motherhood. After we seemed to be in the clear, both Pili and I had this weird feeling. One that neither of us could really articulate at the time. Yes, we were absolutely relieved that I didn't turn out to be pregnant, but there was more. Why was I so relieved? Why was I so viscerally upset with myself when I thought I was going to have an abortion? Why did I feel this incredibly violent dread and shame? I don't think either of us was properly equipped at the time, emotionally, to unpack all of that trauma.

So we didn't. We tried our absolute best to ignore it and

move forward as if it had never happened. Pili and I didn't talk about what had happened, and for months, I didn't tell anyone. I never hide anything from my family, especially from my mom and sister, and yet I hid this from them. I swore to myself that I would never tell anyone, because it wasn't anyone's business. And it didn't even end up being real, so who cares? Running from your problems never works, but I tried my fucking hardest to. Turns out, I'm not that fast.

After lots of therapy and self-reflection, I know now why I struggled so much, and still do, with this experience. I was ashamed, for many reasons. Ashamed that I got myself into that position, ashamed that I had to handle it in secret, ashamed that I wanted to get an abortion . . . but most of all, I was ashamed because it finally confirmed for me that I never wanted to have children. And coming to that realization was the worst feeling in the world, because now I *actually* knew. The truth haunted me so severely, it began to transform my relationship with my boyfriend and my family for the worse. After a couple of months of hiding these feelings and wrestling with them internally, I finally decided that I was tired of bottling it all up inside.

When I told my mom and my sister the truth about my pregnancy scare, we all cried. We held one another and just sat with our emotions, which I didn't realize I needed so desperately until then. Admitting to my mom that I never wanted to have kids was something I was so afraid of, especially since she draws so much power from being a mother and has created such a wonderful life for my siblings and me. After all, looking up to my mom is what made me even consider gravitating toward inhabiting the "mom" role so much as a kid. When you grow up in a Samoan household, your family legacy means everything, and last names are so incredibly important. As I wrestled with the very real feelings of disdain toward having kids, I felt so much culturally driven shame. All of it was self-inflicted, but I do think it was natural, given how proud I was to be a Samoan person and be a part of the Samoan community. I felt the immense pride of Samoan parents, my own included, when they had a big, beautiful family to represent their name. I felt the love of a giant family, with grandparents and aunties and uncles and cousins galore. How could I admit to my parents that that wasn't going to be the case for our family via my bloodline?

You can imagine my relief and the intensely freeing feeling of finally being able to share an emotionally harrowing experience with the people closest to me. So, during our conversation, when I admitted to my mom that I thought I might never want to have kids at all, she paused for a second and then asked me, "Why do you think that?"

My response was simple but blunt. "Because if even the thought of getting pregnant makes me feel nothing but anxiety and fear, then I think that's a pretty clear sign that I shouldn't have kids." I think the honesty of my answer struck my mom immediately: she knew I meant what I said. And that was all the confirmation she needed, because both she and my dad just want me to be happy. After all, I should've known that part of what makes my mom an extraordinary person is exactly what makes her such an incredible mother—

she responded with complete love and support, as she always has and always will, no matter what I share with her about myself. That year for Christmas, she got me and Pili a gift for our future house with a little note that read, "For when you build your family home. You know, with a couple of dogs." (And yeah, that made me sob, all right? I don't want to fucking talk about it.)

When it came to Pili and me, we finally had a long, overdue, and fully honest conversation about why we were so shaken by that experience. It's ironic, because a pregnancy would've changed everything, and even though it turned out to be a false positive, just the stress and uncertainty of the situation almost changed everything anyway. It took a lot of tears, love, and mutual trust, but we were finally able to come to the conclusion, together, that neither of us wanted kids. We just didn't want to lose the other person if they felt differently. Looking back, this was only further confirmation that we were meant for each other (as cheesy as that shit sounds). Afterward, it felt like our relationship deepened even further. Knowing that we were in full agreement with each other about parenthood removed the final big uncertainty in our ability to imagine our life together. I know now that it's so imperative to be honest in conversations like that with your significant other, but, more important, to be honest with yourself.

I think that this experience was the final weed of internalized misogyny I had to rip out. As much as I supported women being career-centered, or wanting to be anything other than a mother, nothing tested me more than those few hours when

I thought I was going to have to choose one or the other. To know and believe that women deserve the right to choose what they do with their bodies and their lives, *whatever* that may be, is essential to being a feminist. There is no right way to be a woman, only your way.

10

YOU'RE WORTH IT

Is it any wonder that women and femmes struggle with bouts of intense self-doubt, coming up in a society that's constantly asking for the smaller, quieter, more passive version of who they really are? It's hard to remain grounded in positive self-belief when so many of our systems intend to make us feel guilty for actively existing within the margins of this patriarchal, misogynistic, fatphobic, and racist society. In this hypercritical environment, the experience of going through a personal setback can feel like the end of the world.

This is parodied in TV shows and movies for a reason—there's something very relatable about watching the hysterical fallen heroine sobbing with mascara running down her cheeks as she clutches a box of assorted half-eaten chocolates after being dumped, or changes her entire look (which is really just her taking off her glasses) in order to land the guy who abandons her before the prom anyway, or chases after her boss and the HR representative who've just cruelly fired her, only to have the elevator doors close on the tip of her nose. When these negative experiences happen—be they professional, personal, romantic, or otherwise—there is a tendency (and a societal expectation, too) for women to punish themselves. We feel pressured to give in to self-loathing and jump to the conclusion that we've failed and that everything is our fault, without stepping back from the situation to evaluate what actually went down. And even when we are able to recognize the various cultural, societal, and political factors at play in a situation, too often we treat that recognition as the only step we're capable of instead of just the first one. Coming to the realization that we're not solely to blame shouldn't be the end of our plotline, it should be the beginning.

This isn't to say that we should avoid accountability for our decisions, but there is a unique socialization that happens leading women and femmes to automatically take on *more* than their share of responsibility (a lot of times meaning we'll perform the bulk of emotional labor), while men avoid taking responsibility whenever possible (a bad habit they're characteristically excused for). We are so quick to assume that we're exclusively at fault when bad stuff happens that we overcompensate by taking the fall for *everything*, to the overall detriment of our happiness and well-being. Knowing your worth (and holding on to it *even tighter* during setbacks) will save you from the person who is many times your own worst enemy: yourself.

Mine? She's a Virgo. She loves to map, manifest, and execute her goals to perfectionistic completion. She *always* has a plan, and plans for her plans, and a backup plan for those plans, just in case they don't work out. She plans five, six, seven years in advance, if not more. And she *hates* it when the plans fall through, no matter how many times she's reminded that nothing in this life is guaranteed or permanent. The universe laughs in the face of those of us who expect every plan to work out exactly as we mapped it in our heads. So yeah, she and I have been working through a lot, but talking sense into her and not always falling for the meanest possible thought she can come up with in the moment has grown easier over time and with experience.

If there's anything she and I have learned this far into my twenties, it's that sometimes, having all your dreams happen according to plan is just what you need to show you that maybe your plans were shit in the first place. Which is my cue to bring this book back to the beginning and finally tell you the whole story of what happened to me when I got fired.

Even though everyone in my family at the time, including Pili, was living a 1099 lifestyle working for themselves as either a business owner or an independent contractor (and they took every opportunity to warn me that corporate America was cold and it did not give a damn about people, especially people like me), after graduating from college I was still convinced that I wanted the prestige of working for a massive entertainment company with global name recognition. This place had applicants submitting their résumés for open positions by the hundreds, if not thousands, and finally, in the summer of 2019, one of those roles became mine.

As it turned out, all of the hard-earned assertiveness, self-esteem, and confidence I had built up in college could be easily dismantled now that I was the new person in the office. No one at the office wanted to hear that I had ambition to work my way up the ladder or even to advance out of my entry-level position until they arbitrarily decided I was ready and that I had paid my dues. What's more, I slowly began to see how the patriarchal environment I was working in would take credit for my ideas, and then convince me that it was necessary for the overall goal of the initiative. If I was *really* a team player, I would surrender my ideas with no complaints . . . and eventually I would be seen for my work ethic and be rewarded. But would I actually? And when was this supposed to happen?

The panic set in, and suddenly I had no idea what I had gotten myself into. My gut told me that this was wrong, that I wasn't meant to feel this way every time I was at work, but whenever I would talk to my coworkers, they would assure me that there was nothing to worry about. This was just *part of the deal*: I'd earn my way into a huge company, start at the bottom, eat shit for a while, and then start to move up. But let me let you in on a little secret: no one manifests eating shit. And this mentality is straight-up dangerous for women, especially women of color, and especially in male-dominated spaces (which we all know are *most* spaces). I met another woman who shared my title and was shocked to learn she had been in the same role for *eight years*. She had been passed over for promotion so many times that I could see she had stopped dreaming of more for herself, and that validated the gut feeling that I had been having all along.

It ended terribly. Less than a year after I started, I was pulled into a conference room and let go. They listed a ton of reasons for the decision, but the one that they made abundantly clear was their lack of belief in my ability to do what the job required: help build a platform and engage an audience. My imposter syndrome went into overdrive, verbally kicking my ass with self-talk: *Of course they fired me. Everyone I crossed paths with wanted me out. It took two years to get that role—how can I possibly find another position now?* My confidence was at an all-time low, and for maybe the first time in my life, I didn't know if I still believed in myself. Who was I if I couldn't succeed at the goals that I had used for years to define who I was and what I wanted in life?

I know now that my experience was not even unique in the context of corporate America, where profits and satisfied shareholders are valued ahead of workplace morale and the well-being of individual employees. Nevertheless, this was one of the hardest, most emotionally draining experiences of my young adult life, and if there's one thing I desperately wish I'd realized back then, it's this: You cannot be expected to leave your personhood at the door for a corporate job, no matter how much they would like you to believe that is the only way to succeed. You owe it to yourself, always, to assert personal agency. No matter what.

I'll never forget walking out of the office building back to my car on my last day with all my personal belongings in hand. I sat in the driver's seat, clutching the steering wheel, tears streaming down my cheeks, thinking to myself, *What just happened?* It was going to be a long drive home. I called my mom first, as usual, but she didn't pick up. Then I tried my sister, but her phone went to voicemail, too. My dad answered on the first ring. In almost complete shock, I shared with him what had happened.

To my surprise, he was ecstatic. He told me, excitedly, as if he had been holding in a secret, "That was not where you were meant to be, *at all*. This is a pivotal moment for you." Confused, I proceeded to remind him that I had just *lost* my job, but he was dead serious. Though it certainly did not feel that way on the two-and-a-half-hour drive home, or even in the weeks and months to follow, I eventually learned he was right.

The next day we all went to Disneyland, where they knew it would be especially difficult for me to feel sorry for myself. I admit that it helped take my mind off the traumatic firing I'd just endured. My mom even bought me a mug in one of the gift shops to commemorate the moment. She told me, "This is to remind you daily that you are destined for greatness. Something ten times greater is waiting around the corner for you. I can feel it." Though I was still skeptical, I secretly began to consider the possibility that maybe my family was right. Maybe there would be a day in my not-so-distant future when I'd look back on this experience from my new and improved professional life and smile. Even if thinking about it felt like an indulgence I didn't deserve, it was comforting to begin to consider that option.

Two weeks later, the world shut down. Covid. Without any of the normalcy of a day-to-day routine of going out for a

coffee or to hit the gym, get groceries, or meet my family or friends for dinner, all I could do was turn over in my head the negative feelings that accompanied losing my dream job. It felt like all of my plans had gone to shit, and I could not see a way out of what felt like a nightmare scenario.

But I had no shortage of time on my hands to think, and started to gently remind myself that my job title was not the most important thing in the world. I still had so much to be grateful for, especially now, and that was easy to see. I had a loving family and a home I could always return to if needed. I had a support system that provided me with options, and for that I was damn lucky. My pain had everything to do with the fact that I had tied my *entire* goddamn worth to a job. My confidence was shaken, and I was having a severely hard time admitting to myself that what I had built up in my mind to be the stepping stone for my dream life was, in fact, just some stupid job.

Your work does not define you. I don't care if you're an entry-level person working for peanuts like I was, or a multi-hyphenate who runs several successful businesses. Your job is *never* going to be the most important part of your life, or the sole thing that brings you joy and reminds you that you're alive. Those moments only happen in life, not work, and that's why there always needs to be balance. Ask me today, and I'll be the first to swear that jobs and corporate structures, just like awful men, will suck the life out of you. They'll drain you of your emotional and spiritual energy, make you question your value and self-worth, and if they end poorly? They'll convince you that it was all your fault. But in 2020, when I

was still going through it and my self-esteem was utterly shot, I was only placing my self-worth in my external accomplishments. I had a half dozen family members telling me repeatedly that I was so much better than the job I had just lost, and I *still* wanted to punish myself for letting it chew me up and spit me out that way.

When you're at the top of your professional game, work can feel so utterly satisfying and validating that it convinces you it's a source of fulfillment and meaning in life. But the workplace is fickle, and no one stays on top forever. There *will* be disappointment, there *will* be conflict and turmoil, and the only certainty in this life is uncertainty. The sooner you can recognize that, the sooner you can begin to detach your self-worth from your successes and setbacks alike.

I had given so much of myself up in order to take the opportunity—the hours I spent sitting in traffic on my commute added up to days if not weeks of my life. Pili and I rarely saw each other, and we were essentially ships passing in the night for the better part of a year. I made the job my first priority because that was what the job had asked of me, and without asking myself what I needed from me, I made the major mistake of failing to assert and protect any boundaries of my own.

It was easy for me to let that happen because I didn't actually even know what my boundaries were back then. I had spent so much time just focused on landing, and hopefully keeping, the job, that I didn't actually have a plan in mind for how I would balance that job with anything else. Figuring out my needs outside of my work and setting my boundaries accordingly has been the most important process in reclaiming

my self-worth over the last few years as I found my way back from this significant professional setback.

Back in college, I would share rants with my friends on Snapchat similar to what I post now, whether they were about schoolwork or a guy that pissed me off, but I put the hobby on hiatus once I started applying for jobs, out of fear that my posting could hold me back from certain opportunities. I couldn't risk being a clown online anymore, now that I had my degrees and could finally put to good use the gender-neutral name my parents had given me *specifically* to help land job interviews, especially going into the sports industry. Besides, I assumed I would likely need to make room in my online presence for media clips and a professional sizzle reel instead. But now that I was fired and my future job trajectory was unclear, I was over it. So I did what every good unemployed American was doing: I joined TikTok. If I would never get to be on-screen talent at my alleged dream job with a media conglomerate, at least I could still be on-screen talent *somewhere.*

From the very beginning, there was just something about it that seemed tailor-made to bring out my mojo, and before I knew it, my platform exploded. From my first viral post, to hitting a million followers, to my first profile in *The New York Times,* to being honored by *Time* magazine, it never ceases to amaze me how all this happened literally as the result of being let go from a job on the grounds that I *couldn't* engage an audience. Suddenly, here I was doing *exactly* that, and it all came from stripping away the external forces I couldn't control, finding the will to keep going, and finally putting my most authentic full self forward. Turns out my previous employer was right about one thing: I wasn't cut out for this major sports network. I was destined for something far greater.

If you were to believe the terrible men online, a "callout" is the greatest persecution someone can face, one they have equated to (and I wish I were joking) oppression—when a lot of the time, I'm literally just describing their behavior. Holding a mirror up to them to show clearly who they are, and how ugly it is. And turns out? Misogynistic men really don't like seeing that kind of reflection. I could say the most objective thing in the world, sometimes even repeating verbatim what they spout, and they'll act as if I committed the ultimate hate crime against them. Their reaction to my reaction is always far more concerning, because instead of reacting to the misogyny, they react to me laughing at them.

Look, I'm a big words-of-affirmation girl, and when it comes to misogynistic men and how they treat women and femmes, there's always been one affirmation that sticks out in my head: *I deserve respect.* In its deceptive simplicity, it's a really effective mantra that distills not only why my content strikes a nerve with my community and haters alike, but also my general approach to life.

All it takes to trigger these men is to literally just *respond.* No matter how small you start, it's just important that you try. In a world where some people are catered to all their lives and indoctrinated into believing that they're superior to oth-

ers just because of their race, gender, family wealth, etc.,
sometimes the best response to their behavior is not education. Nor is it patience and empathy (two things they receive
far too much of and that they don't deserve from marginalized
communities). It's laughing in their faces, and loudly. It's applying the same Neanderthal logic and humor that they implement in their daily lives and giving it back to them. This is what
terrible men, racists, rude people, people with biases, cruel
bosses, and pick-mes alike absolutely can't stand. Because at the
end of the day, these people are cowards. They're scared of how
other men would perceive them if they were to stand up for
women publicly. They're scared of any perceived differences
that might cause them to come out of their comfort zone.
They're scared of having to examine the very real privileges that
they have, because it might mean that they aren't special, just
mediocre. But most of all, they're scared to cop to their internalized biases, let alone be held accountable for them.

You all can probably tell by this point that I'm a bitch who
loves to be right (Virgo core), and especially when it's at the
expense of a horrible person. And I *will* make sure they know
I was right, too. When I was a kid and I saw how bullies on
the playground would take advantage of my sister's kindness?
I didn't just say something, I *did* something about it—when
we played house at school and the other kids tried to assign
her the role of the dog, I corrected them, "No, actually, *you're*
the dog. Deison's the sister, and *I'm* the mom." When I got to
college and saw how random men would treat my friends
poorly? I eviscerated them every chance I could so they never
forgot that every single woman they ever had the pleasure of

crossing paths with deserved better than them. And, of course, when I started creating content and realized that the internet was also full of horrible men harassing women and so many others in ways I had never seen before? Repeat after me: I. Said. Something.

Of course, I want to take this moment to acknowledge that there is real violence in this world, especially toward Black and brown people, femmes of all races, and all my friends in the LGBTQIA+ community. In those instances where there is the possibility of real bodily, physical harm, I want you to do whatever it takes to stay safe and stay alive so you can keep on experiencing all the love and joy this world has to offer. I am not advocating for assertiveness or for saying something when it might mean you could be endangering your life, even though it fully sucks that I have to acknowledge that very real possibility at all. Everyone deserves to exist safely and wholly as themselves in this world. And nothing, but *especially* not some random awful man in the wild, is worth sacrificing your safety for.

But for my baddies who are dealing with the more subtle flavor of a death-by-a-thousand-paper-cuts-style prejudice that is unfortunately so pervasive in contemporary society, I encourage you to take that mantra to heart: *I deserve respect.*

For many people, not wanting to speak out is rooted in a desire to not cause a scene and the very real fear that speaking out or standing up for yourself could be mistaken for aggression. And specifically for women, it's rooted in the desire to refrain from being vilified as "uptight" or a "bitch." It's especially upsetting when it is further distorted by racist, classist, homophobic, or transphobic assumptions.

I've been the target of these assumptions and have been called overly aggressive or outright dismissed for what I have to say so many times in my career, but the one experience that really pissed me off was the time when my community told me about another creator who was saying exactly what I was saying and ripping off my entire bit. She stole so many of my jokes verbatim and copied my tone, my cadence, and even my mannerisms. When I went over to her page, I was shocked to see that whereas I was getting death threats and racist, fatphobic insults in my comment sections, the exact same demographic of terrible men was in *her* comments saying things like *You're making some good points*. And, yes, she was a white woman. To be clear, I'm not pissed at her, because I obviously don't think she (or anyone else) should in any way be subject to the same vitriol I have been, but rather at the double standards that men have for women who look like me, versus ones that look like her.

I often joke around about being *extremely* confrontational, but the reason I don't change is because I'm never confrontational just for the sake of it, but always with a clear purpose and intent. Realizing just how much society is stacked against you can make it hard to muster the courage to speak up and be assertive, but what I want you to know is that it's exactly *because* society is stacked against you that it's so important to advocate for yourself. You matter, and you deserve to be treated as such. We need your voice now more than ever.

It's fucking cool and empowering to be able to express yourself and assert agency. This might mean not having to always show up in a manner that is palatable to men. Feeling comfortable being vulnerable at times and strong and secure at others is one of the greatest keys to happiness in life, I've found. Even though I no longer have a boss or anyone else to answer to other than those I have handpicked to be on my team, I remain keenly aware of my own worth as the outpouring of outraged, terrible men flocks to my comments and stitches my videos to rally against me, calling me every uncreative name under the sun. Their feedback means nothing to me because I'm too busy focusing on the engagement from the community I've built alongside people who thank me for giving them the tools to begin the process of unlearning how deeply the patriarchy has been rooted into their brains. Every DM, every comment, and every time someone stops me on the street to tell me that I gave them confidence to leave a shitty situation or stand up for themselves are what keeps me going.

Obviously, losing the job that I thought was meant for me was ultimately a stepping stone to get me to where I am today. That's clear to me now. But even though it was unanimously decided (by everyone *but* me) that it was not where I belonged, it still sometimes worries me when I think about the next young hire who will walk through their office doors full of hope. There are so many systemic issues working against women, femmes, and people of color in the workplace, from lack of benefits and health coverage for entry-level employees, to the gender wage gap and salary compression, to slim opportunities for advancement in this economy. We all need support and someone by our side. We need one another.

Stay resolute about finding community. Make friends

with your colleagues in similar positions who are also young women of color, members of the LGBTQIA+ community, and allies interested in speaking candidly and with transparency about their workloads and salaries. Information is power, and speaking up is the only path to making workplaces more equitable, especially for marginalized folks. The only thing more powerful than knowing your own worth is recognizing and asserting it, together with incredibly talented peers who are there to continue to not only validate your experiences, but also fight for you where they can.

Today my relationship to work is not unlike my relationship to my body—decidedly neutral. I prioritize my mental health in relation to both by no longer allowing myself to weigh the outcome of my accomplishments, or perceptions of my body, heavily against my self-worth. I've found one of the best safeguards in protecting your self-worth at work lies in establishing boundaries. This took me a *long* time to get right, so I won't pretend that it's easy, but even if you're not quite ready to have a conversation with your higher-ups or team about implementing changes to guard work/life balance, it's important to start the process of recognizing how you might be overvaluing your perception of yourself at work to the detriment of who you are with family, in relationships, as part of your community, and in pursuit of outside goals. Because, yes, you can have goals as an adult that aren't solely tied to advancing in your current career, and if that's what you want, I want for you to know that you can have it. If you continue to only dig deeper and deeper, trying to summon energy to give everything you can possibly spare from your personal life back to your job, it's safe to assume that you will burn out.

Work hard, but within reason, and never just to promote some toxic standard of what young and "hungry" professionals should be capable of. Knowing your worth means going above and beyond *for yourself* just as often, if not more often, than you are for any organization or job. There's a reason they don't make it easy for you to figure out the rules. Companies would prefer not to pay you—they love it when people want to work for free, especially if they can exploit your desire to overperform and work your way up the ladder—but turning a blind eye to it isn't ethical or legal on their part. So knowing that they don't and won't fight for you means you have to fight for yourself.

I don't have to tell you that I credit my incredible family for backing me up and believing in me, even when I had nearly stopped believing in myself. The way they all rallied behind me when I was at my lowest is something I am truly so grateful for. They keep me grounded, so I keep them *close*. And I mean *all* of them. I get invited somewhere and I'm like, *Can I get a plus-seven, please?* My family is everything to me, and now that I have the privilege of being able to work for myself, I prioritize getting to spend as much time with them as I possibly can. It's been a whirlwind the last few years and the hustle shows no sign of slowing down anytime soon, but prioritizing boundaries around the time I get to spend with my family brings me immense joy. They are absolutely a substantial pillar in why I've reached success and happiness in equal measure. Any downtime I get is given back to the people I care about the most in this entire world, and nothing feels better than that.

In the years that I've had a public platform, I've received countless comments, DMs, and in-person questions about relationships, jobs, self-esteem, and everything in between. And for the most part, they all boil down to one question: *Where the hell, in a world that does everything it possibly can to keep someone like me down, do I get my confidence?* It's true that over the years I've gained a reputation for my brazen and unapologetic reaction to bigoted men online. But in these messages, I'm often asked what advice I have specifically for people who are at the very beginning of their self-love journey, for whom my trigger-happy outspokenness might seem like an impossible goal. One piece of advice I always give the shy baddies is to start small. If you're someone who struggles to tell another person to their face when they're disrespecting you, chances are you're letting that behavior slide in much smaller ways, too. Correcting someone when they say your name wrong, asking for the right drink order when they accidentally mess it up at Starbucks . . . the list goes on. These are the very baselines of advocating for yourself, so when people ask how they can work their way up to my self-belief, I always encourage them to start here.

We, especially those of us who are socialized as women or who have had to deal with racist expectations surrounding respectability, are conditioned not to rock the boat, especially not over the small things. But over time, that conditional "polite" response becomes internalized, which affects your ability to judge which are the small things and which are the big things, and ultimately chips away at your ability to tolerate—or *not* tolerate—rudeness or disrespect on a much more significant scale.

But I have good news for you, which is that it's never too late to learn how to assert yourself, and that it only becomes easier the more you do it. It's all about the reps—the more you practice, the better you get. While you venture down that path, it's important to remind yourself that there is nothing rude about standing up for yourself. The first time you speak up will be the hardest, there's no way around it, but I promise you that the relief you will feel after will liberate you.

The key to becoming more confident in standing up for yourself lies in tackling the little things first, because they are there to help you begin to *believe* that you should always assert yourself and want the best. Why shouldn't you correct someone who mispronounces your name? Or hands you the wrong drink order? Of course this isn't indicative of their character off the bat, but it is indicative of how you see yourself. Why do you think you aren't worthy of basic respect? Something as simple as a name mishap matters in the grand scheme, and it's important you recognize the significance of advocating for yourself, even in small moments.

From what I've observed, this impulse comes from running on a kind of social autopilot. For example, if you take a sip of your Starbucks order and realize they've given you the wrong drink, your automatic instinct might be to just think, *It's fine! Coffee's coffee!* Maybe you're already halfway out the door, and you've already resigned yourself to settling for any drink at all, and it doesn't matter if it's the one you paid for.

Babe, no! Turn around, go back to the register, wait for the barista to finish what they're doing, and tell them—politely, of course—*Excuse me, but this isn't what I ordered*. You're not being rude, you're advocating for yourself, because you deserve it.

Imagine: If you heard about your friend passively accepting disrespect or sexism from her boss, what would you do? You'd stand up for her and tell her she deserves better, and that they'd have to physically restrain you from giving her boss a piece of your mind. If your friend received an incredible opportunity but was having imposter syndrome about taking it, what would you do? You'd tell her to definitely pursue it, because she's smart, hardworking, and creative. If your friend was looking at a picture and could only point out her perceived flaws, what would you do? You'd tell her that she looks beautiful and that she's perfect exactly as she is.

So why is this emotional capacity never something you offer to yourself? Why do you think you aren't worthy of the love and support you so freely give to others you care about?

I've seen the people who are the most selfless, most forgiving, and most supportive toward their friends and loved ones turn around and give themselves the hardest time. But just as you would want the people you care about to be able to see themselves as the extraordinary and brilliant individuals you know they are, I hope you're able to extend that same grace to yourself. Once you start the mental exercise of imagining yourself as someone you love and respect, my hope is that it will spark the journey of believing that *you* are someone who deserves that same level of love and respect.

An exercise I like to encourage when it feels like you're about to spiral into a fit of anxiety is to pause, take a deep breath, and literally imagine stepping outside of yourself and seeing your inner child. Imagine they're telling themselves all of these harsh criticisms of themselves as a person, their looks, and everything else in between. Imagine how they would feel hearing you inflict those same harsh words that you impose on yourself? If they were hurt by these words and looked genuinely upset—what advice would you give them? Would you offer them criticism? Or would you hold space for them? Would you dogpile onto the self-doubt, or would you offer them encouragement, support, and love? I want you to practice this exercise and remember how much your inner child needs you. When you have these moments of self-doubt, I want you to see that version of yourself and give them all the love and support you both need . . . because you deserve it.

This is the approach that's done the most work in shifting my own mindset, because, outside of my family, my friendships with other women and femmes are what I value most. They are the ones who woke me up to the failing endeavor of upholding patriarchal standards and instead gave me a new foundation of love, community, and support. Without them, I would not be who I am today. It is so important to me to find, make, and cultivate these friendships. What a privilege life is, having felt the warmth and love of women. I can only hope that y'all experience it as well.

Standing up for yourself is *work*. But learning how could be one of the most rewarding things you do. As with most seemingly impossible tasks in life, it's important to start small and be kind to yourself. I would love it if, after reading this chapter, should you meet someone who mispronounces your name tomorrow, you feel empowered to say, *Actually, it's pronounced like* this. But even if you don't, even if just the thought crosses your mind and you end up letting it slide—that's progress. And so if something similar happens the day or week or month after that, you'll be ready then. And when you are, just keep going!

It's easy for me to believe that you are someone who's worthy of love and respect, and to remind you that you absolutely have the ability to assert and stand up for yourself in a hypothetical situation, but I know it's not something you'll accomplish overnight without practice. It's not something that everyone naturally gravitates toward (most often by no fault of their own), but I firmly believe that on the other side is where you'll find your best self yet. The self who you deserve, and who's so worth it.

11

LIVING OUT LOUD

I want to end this book with the acknowledgment that the journey toward empowering, becoming, and loving yourself is one that is lifelong. And it is a hard road to travel. As much as I talk a big game, the truth is, I still don't have it all figured out. And that's okay. Life is always requiring you to be more vulnerable than you ever have been before, and it's okay to let uncertainty in sometimes. I know just how grueling the work of coming into your own can be, while battling all the expectations and limitations the patriarchy tries to put on you. If you've gotten this far, I know it means you are committed to doing the work of unlearning damaging self-beliefs and rebuilding your own confidence and sense of self, outside of the realm of the male gaze.

And I am so proud of you for it. Because what comes with subjecting yourself to vulnerability, hurt, and uncertainty is the possibility of opening yourself up to so much love, support, and confidence, and the opportunity to find community with like-minded people who see you for who you really are. In turn, that love, support, and confidence in yourself will radiate outward to the people around you.

If you don't have your supportive unit just yet, you can use this book as a tool to start building support within yourself first. If there's anything else you take away from it, please make it this: you are worth all the love and respect you put out into the world, and you are *destined* to receive it. I hope that as you navigate life, you can remember my voice from the pages of this book guiding you to the life you deserve. I hope my words stick with you in life to remind you, always, of how incredible and amazing you are. I hope they serve to remind you how valid your feelings are and how worthy you are of respect. And maybe most importantly: I hope they make you feel brave. My friend Tefi Pessoa (another brilliant content creator whom I love and adore) once told me, "Sometimes when I don't want to speak up for myself, I imagine you doing it. You make me better and sit up a little straighter . . . shoulders back, chin up." I hope after reading this, the next time you encounter a situation where you're being confronted by bigotry, you feel inclined to sit up straight, too.

In so many ways, we are all our own first generation. I know this might sound strange coming from me, as I am so vocal about how much of myself I owe to my family, but what I mean by it is, as influenced as you are by the people who come before you, you also enter into the world and grow within it as an individual. I may carry my parents' lessons within me, but I'm also interacting with the world every day as just Drew.

Every so often, I'll look back on the last few years of my life and feel overwhelming disbelief that I am here. My life is so different from how I could have ever imagined it to be back in 2020, having just been let go from what I thought was my dream job and facing the start of a pandemic . . . and yet I firmly believe this is exactly where I was supposed to end up.

And by that I don't mean TikTok or even this book, but rather the all-encompassing emotional and mental peace I've found knowing that every day I am loudly living my truth and helping others in the process. Building a platform and creating content is just the vehicle for it all. After all, there are many different reasons people start posting online, but for me, personally, it didn't start from a place of wanting to build a career. Since building a platform, I've received messages full of vitriol, that promise violence or worse, all in response to some simple jokes I made about someone who openly platformed their bigotry of their own free will. I've heard the most vile shit said about my race, my body, or how I look, talk, and carry myself. I've faced many different kinds of threats. The fact that I am a young woman of color creating content empowering women and so many other people by making fun of terrible men seems to enrage them. But I am not at all surprised that I get as much hate as I do from horrible men. It's an unfortunate by-product of standing up to bigotry publicly. Plus, I know that at the end of the day, even if I posted content having nothing to do with feminism, I would still receive hate.

Unfortunately, that's just what it's like to exist as a woman in this world. The only difference with my experience is that it's being documented publicly, for all the world to see.

At the same time, I've gotten the opportunity to travel places I'd never been, work with brands and people I've admired for so long, and most importantly, have my rants, jokes, and beliefs connect me to so many of you. And that's what matters to me. That's what keeps me going. When the load of this high-stakes, public-facing job, of the violent and consistent vitriol I receive every single day, feels heavier than usual, I think about you all. I think about those of you who have been so kind and trusting as to share your stories with me and with one another. This is what a community is.

Not to get too spiritual, but something I believe in strongly is the power of manifestation. It's a practice that I would recommend everyone make part of their lives. Everything I've done in the last few years, every new experience, every opportunity, every success, every meaningful interaction, is something that I put into action through my thoughts via manifestation first. It might start with a wish as small as *I want to make one new good friend this year*, or something as big and vague as *I want to find my dream job*. The key to manifestation is being able to identify that desire, name it out loud, and then really allow yourself to imagine it happening with no restrictions. The idea is that you will attract the things that you desire not only because you work hard to attain them, but because you believe you *deserve* them. As women and femmes, we've been conditioned to temper our own dreams and desires even without prompting; otherwise, we may end up bitter and alone, void of any success, happiness, or a person to love us. I'm here to remind you that I am living proof that that isn't true.

This is your life. Don't waste one second of it living for anyone but yourself.

ACKNOWLEDGMENTS

When I was originally approached about writing a book, I wasn't sure if my words or thoughts would ever truly be important enough to be published for the world to see. I think part of my doubt was imposter syndrome, but I think a larger part was that I truly didn't believe my thoughts and feelings were unique enough to warrant being memorialized. And I think that's because I am a proud Samoan woman, born and raised with my Samoan culture, which means I'll probably always attribute my sense of self to my support system, my community, my family. Nothing about me was possible without the people I love, and none of my beliefs would be so steadfast had it not been for them. So, I'm grateful I get to thank and give credit to the people I love and cherish the most in this world.

Thank you to my parents, Noelle and Tait Afualo. I know it seems clichéd (because it is, although that never makes it any less true), but I don't know how I got so lucky to have you guys. Both of you were so young when you had my siblings and me, and although we struggled financially and times were uncertain . . . we never wanted for what we needed most in this world, and that was love. I'm proud to say that my parents are shining examples of people *meant* to have children. Ones who were born to love their children unconditionally. Thank you for believing in me, loving me, and picking me up when I'm down. My unbridled confidence has known no bounds since I could formulate thoughts, and neither of you ever dimmed my light. You both constantly encouraged me to shine bigger and brighter and to never be ashamed of being loud about who I was. Thank you for giving me the tools I needed in this life to truly embody who I was always meant to be. I'm forever indebted to you both, but I'll spend the rest of my life trying to give you just a fraction of what y'all have given me. I love you to the moon and back!

Thank you to my sister, Deison Afualo, and my brother, Donovan Afualo. The best and funniest siblings one could ever have (can you imagine if I was the only funny one?! YUCK). Deison is my older sister and has been my best friend since Day One. The one person on this planet who truly understands me, more than I do myself. The first person I ever defended from bullies and an inspiration to me in so many ways. I love you so much, pal. To my younger brother, Donnie, my first-ever baby, I'm so thankful you came along and completed our AF5. The first person who ever taught me patience and whose imagination I envy. One of the few people I know in this world who is pure and good to their core, I love you so much, buddy. I'm so grateful to exist in a world where my siblings do, too.

To the love of my life, my person forever, Pili Tanuvasa. There's not much I can properly articulate when it comes to how much I cherish you, but I'll never grow tired of saying it. Thank you for showing me what a true, deep, and soul-touching love can be like. I talk about this in the book, but I never thought I would meet someone who truly saw me for who I was. When you saw the light from within me, and how big and strong it burned, you didn't shy away. You didn't run or lash out against it like so many men before. Instead, you basked in the warmth of it. And the feeling was mutual when I witnessed yours. You felt the warmth and you encouraged others to join in because it didn't frighten you . . . it inspired you. And as someone who believed that they would willingly and happily die alone at one point, I'm thankful that the universe had other plans for us. I would find and love you in any lifetime, but I'm grateful I get to love you in this one.

To my team: my agent, Alexandra French, and my manager, Phil Battiato . . . I can't thank you enough for all you've done for me, my career, and even my family. This world and industry can be terrifying and isolating spaces, and I can't believe how incredibly lucky I am to walk through them arm in arm with two of the best people. You guys believed in me far before anyone else did and have always encouraged and supported my autonomy in this business. It's so rare you get lucky with a kick-ass team on the first try, but I'm a Virgo, so my people instincts are never wrong. Thank you for supporting all my rights, and supporting me through my wrongs. I love and appreciate you both so much! To Marc Gerald, my literary agent, as well as Clare Mao and Leah Petrakis, both of whom are also part of this team: thank you! Marc, for your endless wisdom, guidance, and belief. And Clare and Leah, for listening to me ramble on and on for hours/days/weeks/months on end when writing this book. The love, support, and trust y'all have shown me never go unnoticed: thank you.

To Questlove and the team at AUWA and FSG: thank you for the belief you showed in me from the very first meeting. For my first book to be in your team's capable and incomparable hands is a badge of honor I do not take lightly, but I will wear proudly.

Last, to all my beautiful baddies: the ones reading this book. A long time ago, I had a job that truly made me believe that there were no redeeming qualities about me. It stripped me of my confidence, my mental health, and so much more. But one of the worst things it warped was my sense of purpose. What am I worth . . . without that job? At the time, I believed nothing at all. And I'm happy to report that *you* all are the reason I don't feel that way anymore. Beyond accolades or recognition, one of the biggest aspects of this job I am grateful for is my sense of purpose. You all give me purpose. You inspire me. Drive me. And love me unconditionally . . . and because of this gift you gave me, I now know that my words *are* enough. Thank you.

A Note About the Author

Drew Afualo (@drewafualo) is a content creator and women's rights advocate. Her writing has appeared in the *Los Angeles Times*, and she has been profiled in *The New York Times*, *Nylon*, and *Rolling Stone*. She was named *Adweek*'s 2022 Digital & Tech Creator of the Year, one of Meta's Creators of Tomorrow, and one of *Time*'s Next Generation Leaders. Afualo has covered the red carpet at the Academy Awards and hosts the Spotify-exclusive podcast *The Comment Section*. *Loud* is her first book.